best of office

INTERIOR DESIGN BEST OF OFFICE

EDITOR IN CHIEF
Cindy Allen

EXECUTIVE EDITOR
Jen Renzi

SENIOR DESIGNER
Karla Lima

DESIGNERS
Selena Chen
Zigeng Li

EDITOR
Kathryn Daniels

MANAGING EDITOR
Helene E. Oberman

CONTRIBUTING WRITERS
Danine Alati
Liz Arnold
Damaris Colhoun
Monica Khemsurov
Anita Rosepka
Stephen Treffinger
Athena Waligore
Deborah Wilk

DIGITAL IMAGING
Igor Tsiperson

PRODUCTION
Sarah Dentry

BOOKS DIRECTOR
Selina Yee

PRODUCTION MANAGER
Christopher Havel

MARKETING DIRECTOR
Tina Brennan

MARKETING ART DIRECTOR
Denise Figueroa

Library of Congress Control Number 2011932700
ISBN-13: 9780983326328
ISBN-10: 0-9833263-2-0
Printed in China
10 9 8 7 6 5 4 3 2 1

INTERIOR DESIGN

INTERIOR DESIGN MAGAZINE
360 Park Avenue South, 17th Floor, New York, NY 10010
www.interiordesign.net

SANDOW.
Brands Powered by Innovation™

SANDOW MEDIA LLC
Corporate Headquarters
3731 NW 8th Avenue, Boca Raton, FL 33431
www.sandowmedia.com

foreword
by Cindy Allen

How do you design the office of the future... today? Now that nine-to-five's passé, can we envision a new workplace that boosts productivity while promoting well-being for all? From my soapbox, I say, "Yes!" And we prove it by shining a spotlight on the shifting realities designers face, showing myriad savvy solutions and, most important, proving the value good design can bring to the wild world of the office.

I'm delighted to present *Interior Design Best of Office*, the third volume in our expanding series (*Best of Year* and *Best of Hospitality* started it off). In the following pages, you'll see what boundless imagination and enormous commitment can do. The result is a rich portfolio of—count 'em—64 projects spanning 10 countries and 31 cities, created by 40 of the world's brightest architects and designers: both emerging stars and industry heavyweights.

The big news in office design is, we're talking *big* business. Our annual Giants research found that in 2011, the top 200 design firms worked on a staggering 21,000 office projects worldwide! Fees climbed to nearly $1 billion ($989 million, for sticklers), and a whopping $6 billion's worth of fixtures and furnishings were specified. And the studios expect to handle roughly the same number again this year.

Benefits are massive on the client side, too. In recruiting, retaining, rebranding, and improving employee health and job satisfaction, design's value to business keeps growing exponentially. The solution for Ogilvy & Mather, by M Moser, as it consolidated its Jarkarta office? To create a spa-like experience. On the flip side, Montroy Andersen DeMarco devised a 24/7 work-place for New York's Innovation Interactive. Cuningham Group Architecture helped Wisconsin's Epic Systems go green—grazing horses and bright red barn included—while IT staffers collaborated with Francis Cauffman on a new Maryland office for W.L. Gore & Associates, a fixture on *Fortune's* "100 Best Companies to Work For" list.

So, kick back and enjoy the view, but not for too long. You've got work to do!

best of office contents

media

Want the scoop on cutting-edge office design? Read all about it right here. From ad agencies to TV networks, these newsworthy spaces share a funky vibe and youthful spirit befitting the work they're designed to support. Staying connected—to the world and one another—is vital for media staffers, who demand features like high-tech meeting rooms and collaboration-sparking benching systems. Energetic communal spaces need to be counterbalanced by chill-out spots; thus the preponderance of breakout areas, decompression zones, and game rooms. *These offices work hard and play hard, too.*

J W T

IA Interior Architects

JWT, ATLANTA

In designing the southeastern regional headquarters of this global communications agency, IA had the opportunity to tell a story about a client whose stock-in-trade is, well, storytelling. The overarching narrative? Blue-sky thinking.

Because the client's nonhierarchical corporate culture embraced open workstations, the layout could take full advantage of light streaming in through floor-to-ceiling window walls. Similarly, the fluid circulation path is dotted with some 40 informal breakout areas and 22 meeting rooms, which are enclosed by white-glass panels that can be used as dry-erase boards. Cladding the central facilities core are bamboo panels embedded with interactive screens and LED displays showcasing the latest JWT projects. Bamboo also accents casegoods in the airy office zones, appointed with linear work surfaces.

Connecting the two levels is a 14-foot-wide staircase, enclosed by glass on one side and oxidized steel on the other. It descends from reception—kitted out in a mélange of sculptural furnishings—to a café and bar area that has a cabana-like flavor. For staffers working on the U.S. Virgin Islands tourism account, it's a real aid: They can lounge with a view of the open sky, then close their eyes and dream up copy about soft sand on a sunny beach.

From left: Behind the reception desk is an installation of Ronan and Erwan Bouroullec's Clouds, textile-covered tiles connected by specially designed rubber bands. Pendant fixtures further illuminate an already bright breakout area. Stools pull up to the lower-level café bar, set against a fabric-clad wall hung with video monitors. ➤

1 STAIRCASE

2 RECEPTION

3 CONFERENCE ROOM

4 WORKSTATIONS

5 RESTROOMS

0   10   20   40

50,000 sf
Renovation

Clockwise from opposite top: Reception's sculptural seating and stools by Charles and Ray Eames can be viewed from either glass-enclosed conference room. Screens are embedded in bamboo panels cladding the facilities core. Bamboo also embellishes runs of filing cabinets in the open-plan work area. A cozy lower-level lounge under the oxidized-steel staircase. Felt-lined walls provide display space in a conference room. Mesh globe pendants add polish to a concrete-floor lounge area.

PROJECT TEAM JULIO BRAGA, JOHN AZINARO, HAEYOUNG SHIN, ALI UCER, SOPHIA YUN, ALEX SARRIA, ANGELO LEBRON, GRETCHEN LOTZ, ALEXANDRA MILLER

PHOTOGRAPHY ERIC LAIGNEL

www.interiorarchitects.com

M Moser Associates

OGILVY & MATHER, JAKARTA, INDONESIA

Having its locations scattered across the city was stifling the internal communications of this advertising giant and making for a less-than-seamless client experience. So Ogilvy & Mather consolidated operations in a single office—two floors of a commercial high-rise—and enlisted M Moser Associates' Kuala Lumpur team to give the interiors a modern but distinctly Indonesian spin.

The designers' intensive observation period yielded ample information about the firm's working methodology. Among the insights was the need for two types of space—one open, the other more enclosed—as well as a multipurpose area that could host everything from town hall–style meetings and meals to ad hoc tête-à-têtes.

An expansive reception area flanked by meeting and conference rooms was designed to evoke a Balinese spa. Local timber was used for the raised floor, the base of an enormous glass desk, and the boardroom tabletop. Nearby, a newly installed staircase leads from the 11th-floor lobby to the 10th-floor café, where a range of settings allow for varied interactions. Even the workstations were made for collaboration: Employees sit at bench-style desks along the perimeter, where they can take advantage of light and views. When privacy or just relaxation is desired, staffers can repair to a circular pod enfolded in sliding mesh panels—or to one of the breezy daybeds lining the window wall, cocooned in drop-down curtains.

Clockwise from left: Silk fixtures form a focal point above the newly created staircase. The stair incorporates bleacher-style seating to encourage impromptu chats, while a slide offers rapid transport between floors. An open-sided breakout area features bench seating. The faceted shell of an 11th floor collaboration space is sheathed in veneer; flooring segues from local timber to dark stone arranged in a herringbone pattern.

28,027 sf
2 floors

1 RECEPTION

2 MEETING ROOMS

3 CONFERENCE ROOM

4 POD

5 DISCUSSION AREA

6 PRIVATE OFFICES

7 WORKSTATIONS

0   10   20   40

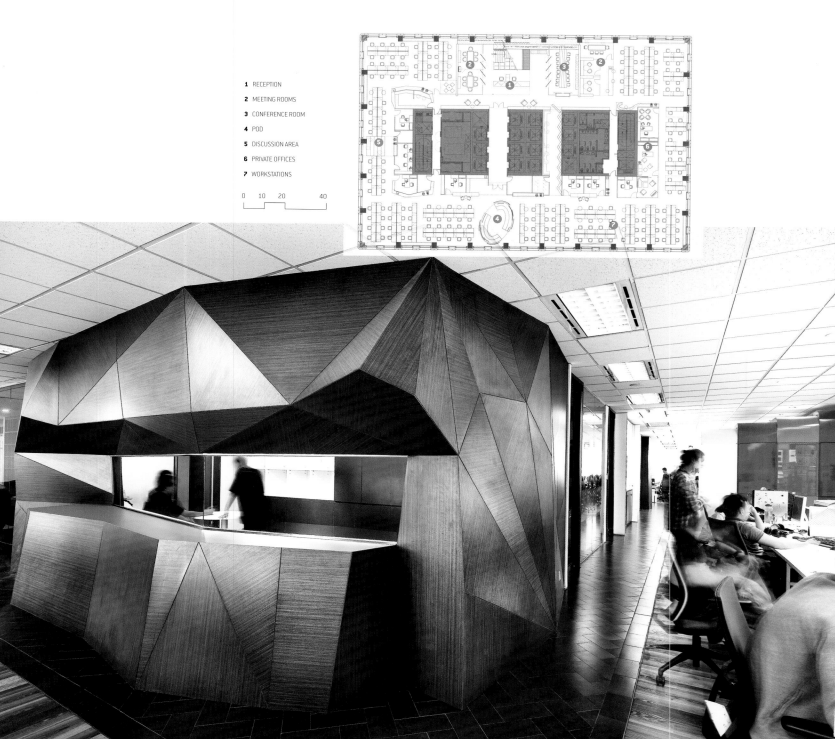

PROJECT TEAM ADRIAN SYMONS, RAMESH SUBRAMANIAM
PHOTOGRAPHY JACK SHEA
www.mmoser.com

Architecture + Information

HORIZON MEDIA, NEW YORK

With offices spread over nine floors in three Midtown buildings some ten blocks apart, Horizon Media lacked both a consolidated headquarters and a cohesive visual identity. Not ideal for a media-buying company whose mission statement is "Making meaningful connections between people." The client found the perfect setting for employee unification in a former printing building downtown. With panoramic views, abundant light, high ceilings, and a raw concrete shell, it was an ideal framework for the inventive culture Horizon wanted to convey.

To reinforce the notion of connection, Architecture + Information chose shared areas and open stations over glass-front private offices. The firm also linked the three

floors with a straight-run staircase that slices through the center of the floor plate. From it, one sees into conference rooms, casual meeting spaces, and work zones.

On the lowest level, a freeform seating area called the "dunes" invites staffers to congregate for motivational talks and presentations: activities that in the past necessitated renting outside space. A 50-foot-long media wall displays the agency's current projects while tracking Internet traffic, the stock market, and other metrics, graphically affirming the client's commitment to innovation.

Clockwise from left:
An open meeting space on the 14th floor is defined by angular custom benches veneered in spalted maple; the wood was sourced from felled trees in Vermont. Reception's media wall can be glimpsed from below thanks to a glass border on the floor. The central staircase terminates at the "dunes," a polished-concrete seating area. The boardroom's ten-monitor screen retracts into the ceiling. The board-room and main presentation room overlook a double-height space whose ceiling is also clad in spalted-maple veneer. Another view of the media wall.

20:80 office-to-workstation ratio

PROJECT TEAM DAG FOLGER, BRADLEY ZIZMOR, SOMMER SCHAUER, ANASTASIA AMELCHAKOVA, AMY MIELKE, PHIL WARD

PHOTOGRAPHY MAGDA BIERNAT

www.aplusi.com

You won't find any scooters careening down the halls of Innovation Interactive's new headquarters, which occupy two full floors of Tribeca's historic AT&T Long Lines Building. Nor is there anything resembling a graffiti wall or beanbag chair. Yet the architects at Montroy Andersen DeMarco did make subtle concessions to the fact that like any rapidly growing digital marketing firm with a youthful staff, the company needed an interior that would cater to the never-ending workday. Its communal lounges feature pool tables and laptop bars; walls are coated in whiteboard paint for impromptu brainstorming (and thus scrawling) sessions; and industrial-steel accents, polished-concrete floors, and hip, loft-appropriate furnishings give it the feel of a home away from home—at least, the kind of home that most of its employees would likely aspire to live in.

Still, the architects wanted to ensure that any time employees spent in their work space would be maximally productive. There are special training rooms for staffers to learn new software, and a green-screen room aids the company's sister ad agency, Firstborn, with in-house photo and video production. (The office is also home to 360i, a digital marketing agency, and Netmining, an audience optimization platform, which share the same parent company.) Sections of raised oak flooring accommodate the extensive wiring and high-speed fiber optics required to support AV equipment and a 1,500-square-foot data center; meeting rooms incorporate state-of-the-art video-conferencing systems. These are, after all, the kinds of perks tech workers come to appreciate most—long after the pool table's allure fades.

Montroy Andersen DeMarco

INNOVATION INTERACTIVE, NEW YORK

Clockwise from top: The loftlike aesthetic is announced in the elevator lobby, with reclaimed-oak flooring and light fixtures that mirror the canted floorplan. A trio of Alfredo Häberli lounges creates a seating vignette near the glass-wall conference rooms. The angular lighting scheme recurs in reception, where wood flooring gives way to polished concrete. ➤

The flick of a switch renders the double-glazed ionized-glass walls of the conference rooms opaque, assuring that meetings stay private when employees use the lounge. ➤

100,000 sf
Whiteboard paint covers 80% of the walls

"High design meets high tech in this space, which was built to work hard and play hard, too"

—STEVEN ANDERSEN

1 ELEVATOR LOBBY

2 RECEPTION

3 TRAINING ROOM

4 CONFERENCE ROOMS

5 EMPLOYEE LOUNGE

6 PRIVATE OFFICE

7 WORKSTATIONS

0   20   40   80

Clockwise from left: Mixing work and play may be encouraged, but the spaces don't need to look identical: Bright colors and expressive lighting fixtures differentiate public spaces—such as the employee lounge—from work zones. A breakout area services private offices. Large sliding-glass doors on perimeter offices let plenty of light pass through; the portals also accentuate extraordinarily high ceilings (some reach 18 feet). Frosted glass and translucent panels allow these offices a measure of privacy.

PROJECT TEAM STEVEN ANDERSEN, TANYA NAUMOVA, DANIEL TEREBELO, AJAY WAGHMARE, MARIANA PANOVA, STACIA KLUI, SHAUNA DACK

PHOTOGRAPHY PAUL WARCHOL

www.madgi.com

25,092 sf

HOK

WUNDERMAN, IRVINE, CALIFORNIA

This ad agency wanted an office as creative as the media campaigns it produces for clients like Land Rover and Nokia. Company leadership envisioned a fun, loungelike environment—the opposite of buttoned-up—that would support interaction and brainstorming. Edicts included the use of invigorating textures and colors, low-level lighting (for energy efficiency and atmosphere), and a residential feel. Oh, and noise. Yes, *noise*, but a certain kind—i.e., the activity and buzz of staffers collaborating and thinking aloud.

HOK laid the foundation for innovation with an allotment of under 200 square feet per person and a less than huge budget. Reclaimed-wood treatments, unique lighting fixtures, and exposed ceiling ductwork are among the features that helped set the mood and save money. Cost-conscious freestanding partitions stand in for solid walls, and much of the homey furniture was sourced locally to reduce transportation fees. A Knoll benching system maximizes space in the workstation areas.

Throughout, punchy graphics—some called Art Stops— aim to stimulate ideas and lend youthful exuberance. A large fourth-floor pantry with an enviable run of windows connects to a balcony, making for a relaxed indoor/outdoor aerie; yellow-painted walls augment the sunshine. The space is so inviting that people frequently step off the elevator just to take a look around—and catch the buzz.

PROJECT TEAM PAM LIGHT, CHRISTY WALLACE, NICKY KAPLAN, TIM HINKLE, POPPY PATTERSON
PHOTOGRAPHY BENNY CHAN/FOTOWORKS
www.hok.com

Clockwise from opposite: *Reclaimed-wood walls and a rope-wrapped column warm reception. A punching bag—for venting—awaits use in a meeting space. The wallpaper is a 1970s Vera Neumann design. Efficient space planning in a private office. An antlered "trophy" lends levity to a sun-lit pantry. A wall of empty black frames features a papier-mâché wolf's head. An open-plan collaboration area. Graphics include work by L.A. street artist Sharktoof. The art resources area is a hub for research and inspiration.*

18,000 sf
Renovation

LAUGHLIN CONSTABLE, CHICAGO

Gary Lee Partners

After many years based in a headquarters mostly divided into private offices, the Windy City creative agency Laughlin Constable sought an environment that would better support its egalitarian culture. Gary Lee Partners met the challenge with an energetic and flexible space that allocates real estate by need rather than seniority. To wit: The best views of Lake Michigan and Millennium Park can be had from "war" rooms and informal meeting areas.

An open floorplan, unobstructed exterior vistas, and the liberal use of interior glass maximizes airiness and allows for abundant natural light. The primary accent color is a zingy orange, chosen to represent the energy of both the place and its inhabitants.

Interspersed throughout are gathering spots designed to foster collaborative group work in a relaxed setting. These include a teaming room, whose walls are punctuated with multicolored felt clouds; a kitschy take on the proper English library; and the Midcentury modern room, featuring iconic furnishings (Eames rockers, for one). There is also a lounge—encompassing kitchen, production area, and game rooms—that's made for socializing and brainstorming, with whiteboard walls for impromptu inspirations.

The workstation area awaits those with heads-down tasks to tackle. This well-equipped sweep of desk space, located near the window walls, provides a distraction-free place for focusing...and dreaming up blue-sky concepts for clients.

Clockwise from opposite: Milwaukee-based graphic artist Mike Meyer painted the floors in the hallway, inspired by tattoos; raw ceilings and walls clad in repurposed wood pallets instill a loftlike feeling. One of the diner-style booths intended for more intimate conversations and personal phone calls. A close-up of the hallway floor. ➤

Clockwise from top left: Neutral carpeting anchors the work-station area, reserved for solitary pursuits. The multitasking lounge, complete with kitchen. Reception's orange walls project the personality of the brand. The lower ceiling of the glassed-in teaming room abets acoustics and thus privacy; reconfigurable felt clouds by Ronan and Erwin Bouroullec help absorb sound in the sparely furnished room. Another view of the workstations.

PROJECT TEAM GARY LEE, RANDY ROUCKA, CHANTAL LAPOINTE, TIM SALISBURY, CHLOE LANGEFELD

PHOTOGRAPHY ANTHONY TAHLIER (1–4, 7), WILLIAM ZBAREN (5, 6, 8)

www.garyleepartners.com

Felderman Keatinge + Associates

SHINE GROUP/REVEILLE PRODUCTIONS, HOLLYWOOD

A Universal Studios lot might seem to be pretty prime real estate for three media concerns owned by the same parent company, but their scattered locations created a logistical challenge, curtailing the potential for camaraderie and cohesion between the entities. Then a landmark building with abundant character entered stage left, signaling a new act for Shine Group/Reveille Productions.

Although the redbrick structure was a bit tight for client (and CEO) Elisabeth Murdoch's needs, she and the FKA team were smitten, quickly acting on their instinct that the space was right. Besides the historic angle, the building had exposed ductwork and mechanical systems that lent it a kind of undisciplined charm.

What evolved was "a young people's space," in the designers' words, with moveable privacy panels that make easy rearrangement and personalization possible. The palette is neutral and clean—workstations are white laminate over fin-ply—and the vibe is slightly funky retro. In the process, the designers adhered to a strict budget and timeline and preserved as much of the original building envelope as possible. For example, the sunny courtyard dividing the offices' two wings, now a welcoming palm-treed spot for eating and socializing, once belonged to a motor court.

The synopsis? Glamorous Old Hollywood meets youthful L.A. cool; sparks fly and an architectural star is reborn.

24,910 sf
Renovation

PROJECT TEAM STANLEY FELDERMAN, NANCY KEATINGE

PHOTOGRAPHY ERIC LAIGNEL

www.fkadesign.com

Fitting the programmatic requirements of office, showroom, and entertainment functions within 7,000 square feet was the challenge MKDA faced in creating the New York outpost for HSN, the 24-hour shopping network based in Florida's St. Petersburg. Instead of trying to cram everything into the tight footprint, the team strategically designed spaces for multiple uses. For instance, the reception desk and pantry counter convert to beverage bars, and a retractable glass boardroom wall opens as needed to accommodate events. The designers judiciously utilized precious real estate by creating a laptop bar for hoteling space. Offices lining the perimeter of the L-shape floor plate maximize light penetration via full-height windows and clear glass

7,000 sf
Renovation

MKDA

HSN, NEW YORK

fronts. Cool materials in the form of poured concrete floors and white lacquer surfaces are juxtaposed with warm reclaimed-oak floors and other millwork touches, exuding a modern yet comfortable aesthetic. MKDA integrated client branding and product advertising through 30 display monitors streaming live broadcasts and floor-to-ceiling Duratrans light boxes featuring ads and graphics.

"HSN wanted this office to reflect its DNA and culture but not replicate the Florida home base," says creative director Edin Rudic. As a result, he adds, "we created something here that's appropriate for New York." In other words, the vibrant space is perfectly suited for the city—and network—that never sleeps.

PROJECT TEAM MICHAEL KLEINBERG, JOHN GIUSEFFI, EDIN RUDIC, MICHAEL CINKEWICZ, BRIAN FELDMAN, ANDY SHELDON, MINDY GROSSMAN, COLLETTE COLLINS, KATE RINGWALD, JORGE FERNANDEZ

PHOTOGRAPHY ADRIAN WILSON

www.mkda.com

Clockwise from far left: A millwork wall unit in the elevator lobby incorporates shelves that showcase and store product and display monitors; sliding barn-style doors conceal additional storage. An HSN logo shines through the mirrored reception desk, which converts to a bar. Stained reclaimed-oak flooring in an executive office introduces a note of warmth. In the boardroom, a retractable wall by NanaWall closes for privacy or opens to annex adjacent space. For events, a mobile beverage bar can be positioned near a Duratrans backdrop featuring branding or product ads; hoteling stations face the window wall.

Tapped by Specific Media to devise a visual identity that could be rolled out to numerous office locations, TPG has now worked continuously for the client over the past four years. The square footage of those projects adds up to over 100,000 square feet of work space in some 12 cities, ranging from the firm's headquarters in Irvine, California, to this project in the West End of London.

The vibrant office is perched on the 10th floor of Central Saint Giles, a colorful multiuse complex designed by Renzo Piano. At more than 25,000 square feet, it is the largest of the digital-media company's international satellites, yet the design was conceived to foster intimate employee collaboration. Comfortable huddle areas are spread throughout, employees work in an open, cubicle-free layout, and a generously sized café serves as an informal hub, with cushy upholstered lounges and groupings of sleek tables tailored to brainstorming sessions.

There are amenities to support both work and play: The office features a full gym as well as Ping-Pong and pool tables. The design is a breath of fresh air—and if staffers find themselves needing a literal one, they can access an all-weather terrace with 360-degree views of London.

TPG Architecture

SPECIFIC MEDIA, LONDON

25,000 sf (office)
425 sf (terrace)

PROJECT TEAM MICHEL FIECHTER, LARRY BERGER, LAURA GHINI, CARLY JACOBSON

PHOTOGRAPHY ROB BROWN

www.tpgarchitecture.com

Clockwise from above: An airy café entices employees with colorful lounges and floor-to-ceiling windows. Central Saint Giles's multi-hued exterior. The café's bar-height eating area is perked up with a bright glossy accent wall. High-back sofas create huddle areas in the open-plan space; interior offices have glass fronts. The reception decor aligns with that of other Specific Media offices by TPG. A trio of Arne Jacobsen Swan chairs surrounds a sleek circular table by the same designer.

fashion & beauty

What's in style? For these clients, it's more than just looking good; it's about working it, too. Trends like democratic layouts, sustainable finishes, copious glass, and the maximization of daylight are fast becoming contemporary-office staples. But equally important for these fashion and beauty companies—whose spaces often function as showrooms, too—are subtle design touches that capture the gestalt of their label: cheeky riffs on brand signatures, couture finishes, decorative elements at once sleek and handcrafted. *They wear it well.*

Highland Associates
and Lissoni Associati

From above: In the pattern-making room, with its backlit glass ceiling, a partition by Erwin Hauer was created with blocks of gypsum pressed in a 1950s mold. The sculpture screens the atelier from the terrazzo-floor reception, where Eames Bent Plywood chairs surround Saarinen tables. ➤

Upon its completion in 1954, Gordon Bunschaft's glass-wrapped design for Manufacturers Hanover Trust signaled a new dawn for bank architecture. More recently, when Elie Tahari took over the fourth floor in the historic Midtown landmark, he aspired to create a state-of-the-art studio that harnessed the structure's groundbreaking spirit. Highland Associates principal Glenn Leitch and Nicoletta Canesi of Lissoni Associati were hired to envision the makeover.

An airy, open layout allows designers, cutters, and pattern makers to work together in a spirit of collaboration. Here every action—a button added, a stitch sewn, a cut made—is executed under Tahari's watchful eye. The building's transparency, revolutionary for its era, turned out to be a boon for modern-day fashion designers, too: The

original glazed ceiling, once restored, proved the perfect device for creating shadowless work surfaces below.

After resurrecting Bunschaft's International Style details, the design team implemented innovative contemporary solutions. New white terrazzo flooring matches the ground level's original mix. Glass panels partition the floorplan. Bench-style workstations help manage density. And continuous steel diffusers installed along the building's east-west axis upped the HVAC capacity.

The showpiece of the renovation is a sculptural Erwin Hauer wall, which separates reception from the studio proper. Woven and punched like an intricate laser-cut textile, it pays tribute to the building's legacy—and its sartorial present.

Clockwise from right:
Casual and cool, the reception area—which serves as elevator lobby and pantry, too—features a Modernica Papa Bear chair, a Vladimir Kagan coffee table, and a bar and stools by Boffi. Thanks to new ductwork, oversize Deglas panels, and properly spaced T8 fluorescents, the conference/fitting room's original ceiling meets modern demands. Communal benches in the work spaces are by Unifor. Starphire glass panels partition the senior designers' offices, furnished with Unifor tables and shelves and Eames chairs.

PHOTOGRAPHY ADRIAN WILSON

www.highlandassociates.com
www.lissoniassociati.com

15,000 sf
$2 million budget

1 RECEPTION

2 MEETING ROOM

3 PRIVATE OFFICE

4 STUDIO

5 PANTRY

0   10   20   40

Calvert Wright Architecture |
Spatial Discipline

DNA MODEL MANAGEMENT, NEW YORK

At DNA, Vitra booking tables and minimalist aluminum shelves displaying head shots give off the cool air one expects of a powerhouse modeling agency. But the library's crackling slate fireplace and punchy throw pillows on plush black sofas lend an unusually down-home family vibe. That's because firm principal Calvert Wright designed the welcoming space to reflect the personalized care DNA offers clients like Linda Evangelista, Natalia Vodianova, Amber Valletta, Chandra North, and Stella Tenant, who consider the Chelsea office their home base. He also aimed for a green sensibility: The library and an informal conference room are adjacent to a lush LED-lit terrarium planted with cypress, sumac, and grasses. Skimming this

leafy grove, a steel stair with ipe railing ascends to a roof deck whose wicker seating encourages drop-ins to chill out.

A combination of open and semi-open work spaces— plus private offices with multiple entries—achieve a similarly laid-back and fluid atmosphere. Low partitions at a consistent 7 ½-foot height abet airflow and offer an uninterrupted view of the loft's wood-beam ceiling. In light of the modest $65-per-square-foot budget, Wright embraced the opportunity to reuse the 19th-century yellow-pine joists that were cleared to make way for the terrarium. Repurposed as doors, benches, tables, and sofa frames, they were treated—as was the refurbished floor—with tung oil, in keeping with DNA's emphasis on natural beauty.

Clockwise from top: The agency's signature red-orange hue crops up in the library's Marimekko fabrics as well as the USM cabinets; Quaker Clear black slate quarried within 100 miles of New York City clads the fireplace surround and the terrarium's west wall. Near booking tables lined with Herman Miller chairs is a pine-backed niche displaying model cards on suspended aluminum shelves. Sails shade the roof deck, where ipe planters contain fragrant creeping rosemary.

6,500 sf (office)
1,500 sf (roof deck)
465 sf (terrarium)

PROJECT TEAM CALVERT WRIGHT, FABIAN BEDOLLA
PHOTOGRAPHY BJÖRG MAGNEA
www.spatialdiscipline.com

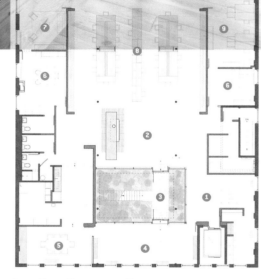

Clockwise from above: The eco-friendly fireplace minimizes the need for fossil fuels in cool weather; cast-iron columns and steel beams were coated with zero-VOC linseed oil. Black slate paves the terrarium. The conference room accommodates meetings at a custom pine table crafted from joists salvaged in the renovation. The terrarium's doors and vents create a chimney for natural breezes, helping cool the space in summer months. Deciduous and coniferous species are focal points both inside and out.

0   10   20   40

1 RECEPTION
2 LIBRARY
3 TERRARIUM
4 CONFERENCE ROOM
5 LUNCHROOM
6 PRIVATE OFFICE
7 PRIVATE CONFERENCE ROOM
8 OPEN WORK AREA (ART AND BOOKING)
9 ADMINISTRATION

Ted Moudis Associates

COTY, NEW YORK

A venerable beauty house in search of a major office makeover ends up in a skyscraper so revered, it was named America's Favorite Architecture in a recent AIA poll: the grand, iconic Empire State Building.

Ted Moudis had an edge even before the site was chosen—he'd designed Coty's previous offices. Still, renovating in a National Historic Landmark posed unique challenges. The ceilings were low and the large building core resulted in long, narrow floor plates, limiting some workstation runs to one row.

Not that you'd know. The largely white rooms feel expansive. A plethora of light fixtures create the impression of a natural glow, even in inner areas. Accents of gold and avocado appear here in the form of a partition or an

Egg chair, there in a round rug or molding trim. Reception seating suggests a hybrid Midcentury modern–Sixties aesthetic; the sleek desk beside it provides a contemporary counterpoint. Throughout, handsome dropped-ceiling elements add interest while masking ductwork.

In many cases, the firm improved on details repurposed from the former space. Vitrines showcasing company products hit a technical snag—halogen bulbs heated up so quickly, they blew transformers. This time a lighting consultant recommended LED puk lights; problem solved. And 21st-century update accomplished.

Clockwise from opposite: Behind the wood-faced reception desk, an LED logo wall lends elegance—and the color can be changed. Vitrines displaying Coty products line a long hallway. A counter surrounded by sculptural barstools beckons groups to share meals and ideas. The conference room has hidden shelving systems. A vibrant gold divider offsets the white walls and furnishings of the café hub, illuminated via a mix of recessed, flush-mount, and pendant lights. Open workstations abut glass-walled private offices.

PROJECT TEAM TED MOUDIS, CHRISTOPHER SAVOGLOU, CESAR ROBLES, PHILIP FIORILLO, JACQUELINE BARR, LUIS VALCARCEL, ERICA GOODIER

PHOTOGRAPHY ADRIAN WILSON

www.tedmoudis.com

87,451 sf
14th and 15th (of 102) floors

50,000 sf
Renovation

Highland
Associates

ELIZABETH ARDEN HEADQUARTERS
STAMFORD, CONNECTICUT

Firm principal Glenn Leitch knew Elizabeth Arden's history well when he was hired to renovate its Stamford office: He had previously revamped, among a variety of projects, the label's New York flagship. Here, the architect made his mark with grand gestures that incorporate iconic elements from the client's corporate branding. Most striking is a serpentine feature wall fronting a pair of conjoined meeting rooms. Filling rows of perforations in the wall's acrylic panels are 8,400 makeup brushes customized with red handles.

Product is showcased constantly, underscoring that this site is home to the company's research-and-development arm. Scattered about are fragrance bottles, allusions to Elizabeth Arden's lucrative licensing partnerships. One chandelierlike installation, above the red reception desk, was created with some 150 empty flacons of Britney Spears's Believe, fitted with LEDs. The canted glass walls enclosing meeting rooms replicate the angles of various bottles; transparent colored film transforms those spaces into giant gemstones of sorts.

On the glass fronts of "drop-in" offices—which are provided to anyone needing privacy for a phone call or to catch up on work—vision strips incorporate the company's Red Door logo. It's one of those small touches that drive home a larger point: Even if a company trades in cosmetics, its renovation must be more than skin deep.

Clockwise from top:
A signature Arden face surveys an office area. Vinyl film surfaces the glass reception desk. A Jeffrey Bernett bench sits in a hallway, outside a meeting room with Pearson Lloyd chairs, a Warren Platner table, and a Ferruccio Laviani pendant fixture. This meeting room shares a front—the makeup-brush wall—with an identical room. ➛

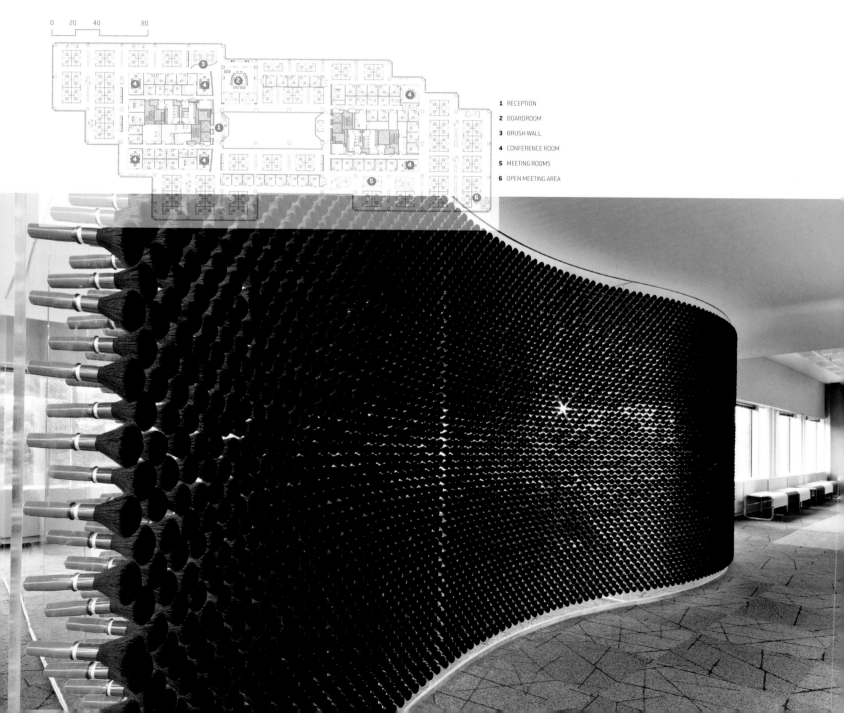

1 RECEPTION

2 BOARDROOM

3 BRUSH WALL

4 CONFERENCE ROOM

5 MEETING ROOMS

6 OPEN MEETING AREA

0 20 40 80

PROJECT TEAM ELIZABETH DEMELLO, MORGAN
GEWANDTER, DEBORAH LORENZO, LEWIS ROANE
PHOTOGRAPHY ERIC LAIGNEL
www.highlandassociates.com

This lively work space expresses the mission of the client, whose name instantly conjures high performance and free-spiritedness. The designers envisioned an open-plan environment that would foster teamwork and cohesion by uniting a quartet of company brands—Nike 360, Nike HK, Umbro, and Cole Haan—under one roof. Since each brand has a distinct identity, the challenge was to devise a scheme that would work for all four.

Using a sports stadium as inspiration, CL3 employed an honest, industrial aesthetic with exposed ceilings, cement columns, reclaimed gymnasium floors and metal lockers, athletic-themed graphics, and invigorating pops of color. The headquarters occupies three levels, with activity flowing around a central core. A pantry and adjacent breakout area on each floor support casual interaction, and contiguous conference rooms can be connected to accommodate companywide functions.

Meanwhile, exclusive "energy rooms" catering to VIP guests display special merch—talk about a slam dunk!

CL3 Architects Limited

NIKE INTERNATIONAL HEADQUARTERS
HONG KONG

PROJECT TEAM WILLIAM LIM, RAYMOND CHOW, JOANNE KWAN
PHOTOGRAPHY NIRUT BENJABANPOT/CL3
www.cl3.com

Clockwise from opposite top: The "energy room," with reclaimed basketball-court flooring, caters to VIP clients. In the similarly floored corridor leading to the latter, Nike sportswear is showcased in a backlit wall niche. In a pantry, aluminum chairs join a spare banquette in the company's signature orange. Metal storage along a hallway brings to mind athletic lockers. Bleacher-style seating and Eero Aarnio Puppy chairs beckon in a breakout area. A zigzagging corridor wall features enormous images of noted sports figures.

55,000 sf
300 employees

Wang

KWOK HANG HOLDINGS
KOWLOON BAY, HONG KONG

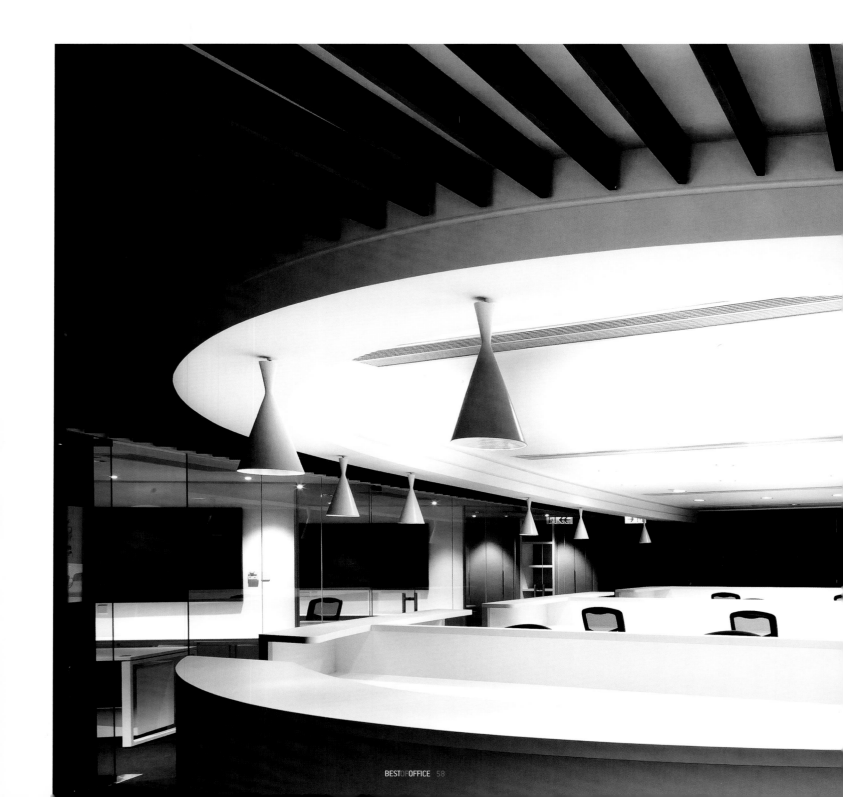

Clockwise from bottom: Conical pendants trace the edge of a sculpted Corian ceiling canopy, which gives a sense of intimacy to the workstations—also Corian—below. An angular opening in reception's faux stone accent wall offers a glimpse into one of the show-rooms. Meetings take place in the comfort of Eames shell chairs, set on a wool-silk area rug. ➣

This headquarters is as chic and sleek as the luxury goods that the client imports from Italy. Wang's commission for the new space coincided with the transition of company leadership from the chairman to his son—and an attendant shift in the corporate culture. Appropriately, the mise-en-scène is forward-thinking yet rooted in tradition, with classic materials treated to novel fabrication methods and rendered in unconventional forms.

The building's oval footprint inspired Wang's sinuous play of lines. Slats of recycled Burmese teak trace an ovoid canopy that defines the open work areas. Glass-walled private offices and common spaces ring the perimeter, where they have visual access to both harbor views and staff goings-on. Meeting rooms reiterate the sweeping geometries, with shapely ceiling insets that look like faceted eggs; below, round lacquered tables float on overscale tartan-print rugs—a fresh twist on tradition.

Contrasting with these fluid forms are a pair of black-box showrooms at the center of the floor plate. Housing jewelry and shoe collections, both rooms have exteriors clad in a textured plaster wall covering that mimics stone. Such juxtapositions of rough and smooth, raw and polished, were designed to reflect the process of refinement that goes into crafting the exquisite products on display.

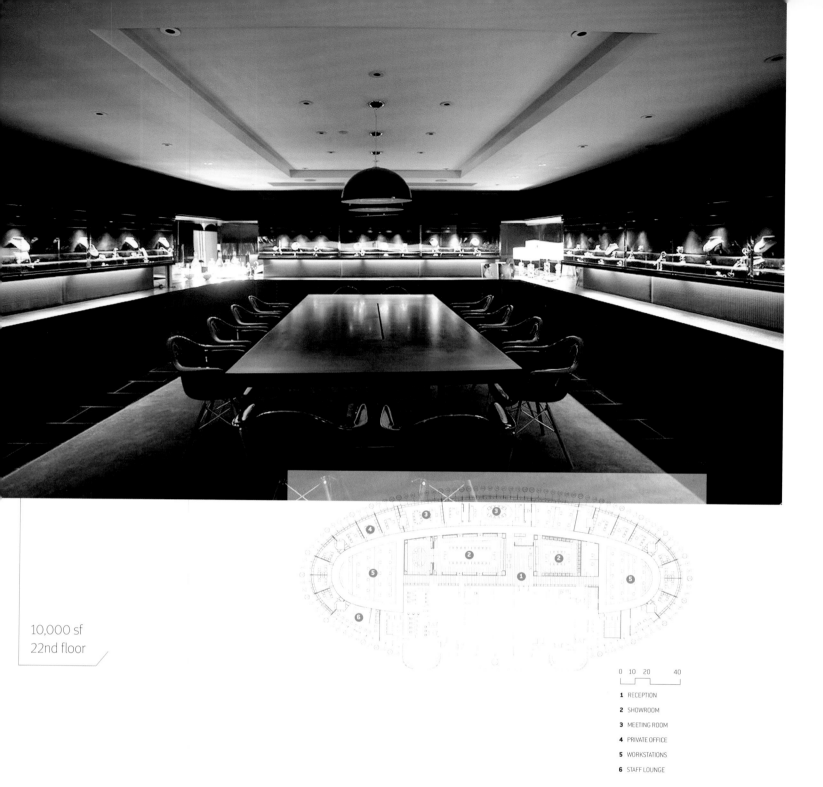

10,000 sf
22nd floor

0 10 20   40

1 RECEPTION

2 SHOWROOM

3 MEETING ROOM

4 PRIVATE OFFICE

5 WORKSTATIONS

6 STAFF LOUNGE

PROJECT TEAM JOYCE WANG, STEFAN KRAKHOFER

PHOTOGRAPHY EDMON LEONG

www.joycewang.com

Clockwise from opposite: A meeting room's faceted ceiling inset is made from aluminum panels coated in automotive paint. A staff pantry and meeting lounge has bar-height seating along the window wall for taking in the view. Spokes of recycled Burmese teak radiate from the ceiling canopy. The jewelry showroom.

Ted Moudis Associates

LUXURY-GOODS MANUFACTURER
NEW YORK

105,000 sf
4 floors

No corners were cut in the making of this stately facility. Careful attention to detail, along with a sense of simplicity and generosity, prevails. Each space stretches out luxuriously—even the ceilings are 25 feet high.

Upon entering reception, visitors are greeted by a massive wedding-cake light fixture recessed in the soaring ceiling, plaster wave walls, and warm pearwood paneling. The first two floors primarily house manufacturing and storage functions: a woodshop, a fabric shop, a warehouse, a security center. Significant public areas exist as well.

The third floor features a conference room for design reviews, private and open offices, and a gym. On the fourth floor are executive offices—with adjoining dining and conference room—and the main café, with its rare uninterrupted views of Manhattan (59th Street Bridge included). Terrazzo tiles, a cracked-glass backsplash, and a custom stone-mosaic feature wall adorn the café, and a 1,200-gallon saltwater fish tank serves as a calming yet ever-shifting focal point.

While the Ted Moudis Associates team designed each space to be unique, materials create overall continuity. Sustainability and ease of maintenance were high priorities, as was recycled content and U.S.-based extraction. Furniture in wood, glass, and stainless steel complements the interiors. Energy conservation also took top billing, so the layout maximizes daylight and views for all departments.

In a word? Meticulous.

Clockwise from above: Pearwood paneling and a 6-foot-diameter custom light fixture bring a more intimate scale to reception, with its Crema Marfil marble floors. A stepped ceiling treatment lends gravitas to the lively employee café. Full-length windows line the perimeter of the workstation zone. A series of pendants and color-changing LEDs over wave walls mark the elevator entrance. The wide-open woodshop and laboratory space.

PROJECT TEAM TED MOUDIS, CHRISTOPHER SAVOGLOU, PERRY LUONGO, DOUG WRAMAGE, LORENZO CALIGARIS, JOHN FERRANTE, MIDORI TAKADA, DAVIDE PLANTERA, JACQUELINE BARR, MONICA LARSEN WETHERELL
PHOTOGRAPHY ADRIAN WILSON
www.tedmoudis.com

ACKRA
TASTY MMI
DELECTABLE
DELICIOU
APPETI
DÉLICIEUX DEL

M-MMM
E
JS
ZING
ECTABLESAVOR

food & beverage

Thirsting for high style? Corporate
headquarters take a delectable turn
in the following foodcentric workplaces.
Bold graphics, witty branding elements,
hospitality-caliber finishes, inventive material
treatments, and ecofriendly elements are all
on the design menu. In these offices, high-tech boardrooms cozy up to top-flight test kitchens; communal spaces suit
brainstorming and entertaining alike. And of course the staff café—or, in some cases, bar—is first rate, with mod
lounge chairs, moody lighting, and stunning views. *Drink it in.*

Johnson Chou

RED BULL CANADA HEAD OFFICE EXPANSION, TORONTO

Outsiders can find it amusing to imagine a workday at Red Bull's Canadian headquarters, with employees bouncing off the walls after quaffing the house brand all day long. The truth is, of course, considerably more prosaic: There's nothing quite so out of the ordinary about working at Red Bull—except perhaps for the walls themselves. The headquarters was conceived by Johnson Chou in two phases: An administrative wing was recently annexed to the office proper, a converted warehouse. The new addition answers the client's request for an inspiring, ecofriendly scheme. "We were challenged to continue the fluid forms of our original design, but via reclaimed materials," says Chou.

Recycled finishes were used to create a series of showstopping interventions. An open-sided box erected from planks of tamarack encloses a new bar/lounge area. When the office hosts events like art openings or parties, a dramatic sliding screen of aluminum mesh seals off a neighboring bank of open work spaces. If employees need quiet, they can retreat to a multipurpose room clad in a wave of sound-absorbing felt. More serious meetings take place in the louvered lean-to that Chou refers to as the "primitive hut." To outsiders, it's simply the boardroom.

Clockwise from left:
A continuous ribbon of reclaimed tamarack transitions between the floor, desks, and ceiling of the open workstations. Visitors enter the new annex from a steel walkway planted inside a red tube; the open bar/ lounge beyond is defined by a sweep of repurposed wood planks. A sinuous wall sheathed in felt disguises an erstwhile elevator core; at rear is the rolling screen that separates lounge and work areas. ➤

11,000 sf (phase one)
5,000 sf (phase two)

In a corridor that leads past the "lean-to" boardroom, an aluminum-mesh screen and random-pattern felt-strip wall cladding instill a raw, industrial-chic vibe.

Clockwise from left:
One of two zones
populated by open
workstations. In the
bar area, moody black
granite contrasts with
roughly textured
tamarack planks.
The boardroom
alternates walls of
felt, blackboard, and
wood strips, the latter
meant to mimic the
effect of light filtering
through branches;
a millworker crafted
the table from a
cherry tree harvested
on his property.

PROJECT TEAM JOHNSON CHOU, SILKE STADTMUELLER, ANNE EHLERS,
ORNA GHORASHI, SHANT KRICHELIAN

PHOTOGRAPHY TOM ARBAN

www.johnsonchou.com

1 RECEPTION

2 BAR/LOUNGE

3 WORKSTATIONS

4 COPY ROOM

5 LAUNCH ROOM

6 BOARDROOM

7 PRIVATE OFFICES

8 BIKE ROOM

9 SERVERY/LOUNGE

"Our strategy was to set rough-hewn reclaimed woods against gleaming metal finishes to create a work space that's at once earthy and sleek"

—JOHNSON CHOU

When most corporate staffers declare it time for a beer, that means leaving the office and hitting the local bar. Not MillerCoors employees: They have the enviable privilege of simply riding an elevator to the headquarter's penthouse pub, where fresh microbrews spill from gleaming taps. VOA's "beer-land" motif doesn't stop there—a handsome brass brewing kettle, helicoptered to the rooftop for installation, is displayed near a conference room. A replica beer-delivery truck was built off-site and reassembled in the lobby. Finally, each of eight levels is themed, representing a specific product in the company's portfolio.

But beyond paying homage to the High Life and the Silver Bullet, the office is steeped in innovation. The central core of each floor plate, known as the Heart, is composed of fiberglass-walled informal meeting rooms as well as recycling and copy centers. Also factored into the design is the company's eco-consciousness, which won the project LEED Silver certification: The sunlight cascading into the open-plan space saves on lighting costs; 95 percent of construction waste was diverted from landfill to recycling centers; and all systems and equipment are energy efficient.

VOA

MILLERCOORS, CHICAGO

130,000 sf
Completed in 8 months

***Clockwise from
opposite top:*** *Near
the brewing kettle,
a wood-slat ceiling
and recessed lighting
lend intimacy to a
conference room. The
top-floor bar. A central
staircase was made
with reclaimed wood;
the surrounding
well's Cream City
brick matches that
of the original Miller
breweries. In each
floor's Heart, motion
sensors adjust the
lighting level and
color according to
activity. Pendant
and linear fixtures
suspended from a
dark-painted ceiling
infuse the open office
with a loftlike feeling.
The reception desk
and illuminated
ceiling feature were
inspired by the
company logo, a
stylized pint glass of
beer seen from above.*

238,000 sf
LEED Gold

BACARDI HEADQUARTERS
CORAL GABLES, FLORIDA

HOK

The iconic stature of Bacardi's former U.S. headquarters, a 1960s Miami landmark, posed a design dilemma when the time came to relocate. Carry over its Latin-modernist aesthetic to the Coral Gables space, or chart a whole new course? HOK chose a little of both. The firm's plan for the site a few miles south of Miami succeeds on many levels, streamlining operations and portraying each company brand—while still honoring the culture.

A triumvirate of decorative styles references the client's architectural heritage. Art Deco details nod to Bacardi's Cuban roots, expressive curves channel Mexico, and Midcentury modernism bespeaks Bermuda and Puerto Rico. These themes play out in design elements and color accents used throughout; every floor has its own palette.

Bacardi's CEO aspired to build the greenest structure in the city and did: The project earned LEED Gold certification via a heavy reliance on Cradle to Cradle elements and nontoxic finishes. Also, 95 percent of construction waste was recycled or otherwise diverted from landfill. An advanced system reduces lighting levels by 35 percent, as does copious glazing that imbues conference spaces and offices with sunshine and a sense of transparency.

At the workstation level, tech integration and proper ergonomics were key. A new IT infrastructure incorporates VOIP phones and desktop videoconferencing. Fully articulating task lamps and monitor arms, multifunctional ergonomic chairs, and some seriously graphic carpets keep workers happy, healthy, and alert.

Clockwise from above: A glass-enclosed staircase leads to the executive conferencing floor. Artwork in the lobby recalls the façade of the former headquarters, a mosaic mural of azure leaves. A Barrisol stretched-ceiling system brings curves to the lounge, a simulated bar, where a light treatment bears the Bacardi bat logo. A branded wall outside the staff dining room. George Nelson Coconut chairs furnish the faux bar, adjacent to the 14th-floor reception area. Office areas feature bold carpet tiles.

PROJECT TEAM KAREN LEAGUE, TIM BLAIR, ANDY SINGLETARY, JULIA BUSBY, JOHN CANTRELL, KIM SYDNOR, MICHAEL RICE, MARIE MIHALIK, SCOTT THOMPSON, JACY HERENDEEN, ELIZABETH TORRES, KEVIN STRAYER, WERONIKA CICHOSZ
PHOTOGRAPHY GABRIEL BENZUR
www.hok.com

Callison

PIZZA HUT/YUM! RESTAURANTS INTERNATIONAL HEADQUARTERS, DALLAS

Clockwise from above: *Environmental graphics bring verve to the cafeteria. In the soaring lobby, walls of stacked stone lend a quietly rugged feel. A teaming zone's lounge and adjacent meeting room are furnished in a mix of crisp white seating. Reception visually integrates both brand identities.* ➤

Yum! Restaurants International selected Callison to realize its new ground-up global headquarters, which the company shares with its Pizza Hut brand. The all-encompassing project included doing extensive research, scouting potential sites, interviewing employees, and collaborating with multiple consultants. Perhaps the biggest challenge, though, was envisioning an interior for two companies with unique identities, a process the designers likened to putting toppings on a pizza: Elements must be in balance to achieve culinary bliss. Thus a neutral backdrop of clean lines and spare natural finishes against which Callison set brand-specific touches in the form of punchy colors and environmental graphics.

The welcoming and sustainably minded campus houses a variety of facilities: test kitchens, common-use breakout areas, a cafeteria, a coffee lounge, a mock-restaurant training facility, collaborative work environments, and a restaurant-support center. Residential appointments— such as the lobby's hearth and textured stone accent wall—render the ambience more hospitality than corporate.

Collaboration is encouraged via flexible and strategically placed teaming areas suited to casual and formal meetings alike. Thanks to varied seating options, the cafeteria is one of many common spaces that support not only eating but also gatherings ranging from small confabs to company-wide assemblies. Dining and brainstorming take place in the high-tech test kitchens as well, veritable research-and-development labs where new products and recipes are conceived and tested. Good taste, indeed.

173,000 sf
Construction completed in 10 months
Awarded two Green Globes from
the Green Building Initiative

Clockwise from left:
The cafeteria's open-plan layout—which also incorporates outdoor space—accommodates 600-plus employees. A dramatic three-story staircase wends through common areas. In a casual breakout space, a blend of furnishings provides comfort as well as flexibility. One of the state-of-the-art test kitchens. Near a test kitchen's pizza oven, a semicircular bar is the perfect spot for recipe testing.

PROJECT TEAM DAVID CASSIDY

PHOTOGRAPHY CHRIS EDEN/CALLISON

www.callison.com

Perkins + Will

DARDEN RESTAURANTS CORPORATE HEADQUARTERS
ORLANDO, FLORIDA

469,000 sf
Over 88% of construction
waste diverted from landfill

Clockwise from right:
A serene corridor is punctuated by an environmental graphic in Darden's trademark crimson. The central spine, aka Main Street, connects three levels of offices and support spaces. The main entrance and security lobby introduces the crisp scheme and assertive palette. Set in the atrium, the 25,000-square-foot employee dining area features walls enlivened by bold artwork. Open stairwells encourage casual interaction; vibrant imagery reflects the client's corporate culture. In the main lobby, full-height glazing offers views of a half-mile walking trail.

The name Darden is practically synonymous with family-style dining: Red Lobster and Olive Garden are among its six festive chains. The full-service restaurant company's new headquarters focuses similarly on convivial engagement. Set on a 57-acre campus lush with native flora, the facility consolidates under one roof some 1,300 employees who'd previously been scattered between 12 buildings.

The LEED Gold–certified design fosters a sense of community while treading lightly on the environment. In a quest to create a healthy workplace, the interdisciplinary firm deployed ecofriendly features such as a reclaimed-water system, energy-saving HVAC and lighting schemes, and high-performance glazing. Daylighting is maximized: Full-height glass walls coax in sunshine, a three-story atrium is traced by a continuous clerestory, and inboard glass-front offices and workstations afford all employees access to restful views.

An open-plan layout instills airiness and supports interaction between each division's staffers. So do public areas. A monumental staircase encourages casual catch-ups, shared spaces are organized around the atrium (called Main Street), and test kitchens for each brand are adjacent to one another so chefs can swap ideas. Other amenities include wellness/fitness centers, a company store, and—naturally—a top-notch dining facility where employees can get a taste of the relaxed and collaborative Darden culture.

PROJECT TEAM JOYCE FOWNES, DON REYNOLDS, MANUEL CADRECHA, LEONARDO ALVAREZ, EILEEN JONES, CHRISTY CAIN, KIM CHAMNESS, BRIAN ERLINDER, ELLEN YOUNG, CHRIS WONG, ERINN DORNAUS, LEONARD TEMKO, BRUCE MCEVOY, MEENA KRENECK, NANCY SHEA
PHOTOGRAPHY STEVE HALL/HEDRICH BLESSING
www.perkinswill.com

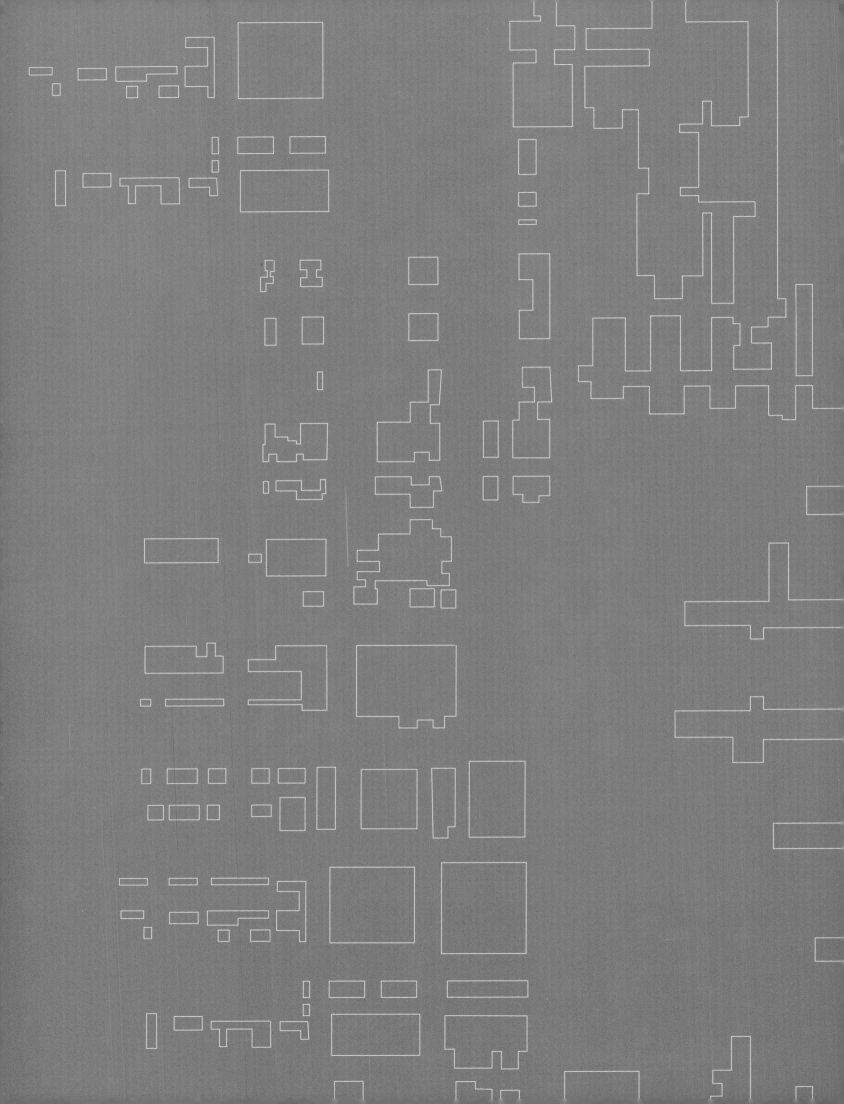

financial

Business as usual? Not so for traders, hedge funders, investment bankers, and the like. On the surface, many of these offices exhibit traditional touchstones: polished-marble floors, formal boardrooms, furniture-design classics. But today's financial headquarters inevitably integrates state-of-the-art technology and modular, open-plan work areas conceived to abet information exchange (and reconfiguration). Amenities such as fitness centers and coffee bars offset the pressure-cooker environment, as do Zen-like accents. *A wise investment, indeed.*

Perkins + Will

TRADING FIRM, CHICAGO

75,000 sf
New construction

Clockwise from top:
Art niches and a rock garden with Japanese spirit stones line a corridor. The lounge area provides respite, with books, movies, and games employees can enjoy. A rippling waterfall, sweeping limestone wall, granite flooring, and natural light in the reception area offer visitors a serene first impression. ➤

"Productive," "harmonious," and "tranquil" might seem unlikely words to use in describing a fast-paced financial setting. But Perkins + Will succeeded in creating such an environment for a privately owned trading firm. The mission for the project team, which collaborated closely with the client, was to design an office replete with organic curves and a flow of spaces that would integrate various business functions.

The designers establish seamless movement among programs that include an open work area with more than 240 desks, a data center, and a large IT support group. Employees can step away from their 120-degree desks

to take advantage of amenities such as a food-service area with a barista, a state-of-the-art fitness center, spalike locker rooms, and a lounge with plush yet sturdy furniture made from leather and durable wools.

Asian influences abound: a Zen rock garden, bonsai sculptures, a koi pond that animates the curved corridors, and Japanese characters adorning bathroom and locker room signage. Illuminated to highlight the art, the office is populated with plate-steel niches showcasing carved-wood Asian sculptures dating from the early 20th century.

The inspired result? A workplace that provides serenity while supporting high-energy activities.

1 RECEPTION

2 FOOD SERVICE

3 MEETING ROOM

4 LOUNGE

5 FITNESS CENTER

6 BULLPEN

7 PRIVATE OFFICE

8 WORKSTATIONS

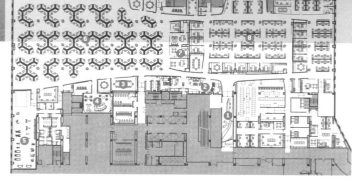

0 10 20 40

Clockwise from opposite: Walls flowing into the open work space are clad in a mixture of plaster and cement. Behind electronically shaded smart glass, the CEO's office is furnished with a Fabien Baron sofa and Jiun Ho chairs. Conference rooms pair lacquered raw steel and paldao-veneer millwork. The fitness center's light fixtures are customized with painted-steel shrouds. Glass-reinforced gypsum enclosures wrap the structural columns in the bullpen, canopied with a maple-veneer soffit.

PROJECT TEAM TOM KASZNIA, TIM WOLFE, ERIC MERSMANN, SARAH KUCHAR, ADY CHU, ROCCO TUNZI, ANDREW WRIGHT

PHOTOGRAPHY MICHELLE LITVIN

www.perkinswill.com

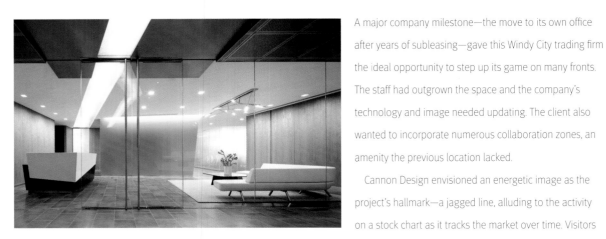

Cannon Design

TRADING FIRM, CHICAGO

32,000 sf
LEED Silver

A major company milestone—the move to its own office after years of subleasing—gave this Windy City trading firm the ideal opportunity to step up its game on many fronts. The staff had outgrown the space and the company's technology and image needed updating. The client also wanted to incorporate numerous collaboration zones, an amenity the previous location lacked.

Cannon Design envisioned an energetic image as the project's hallmark—a jagged line, alluding to the activity on a stock chart as it tracks the market over time. Visitors first encounter the motif when stepping off the elevator: An illuminated ribbon traces a path up the wall and across a faceted metal ceiling before traversing reception and ending at the boardroom entrance.

Roomy trading stations are state of the art, with each accommodating up to 12 monitors. Bench seating lets occupants see one another, as well as the TV at each row's end. These arrangements ensure that a wealth of timely information is always close at hand.

Given that market machinations are notoriously frenetic, Cannon Design also addressed the staff's need to decompress. A large break room—stocked with snacks and games like Wii and Xbox—offers relaxation after the closing bell rings.

With new headquarters, the firm aimed to modernize its profile and boost its ability to attract top talent: Goals, no doubt, achieved.

PROJECT TEAM MEG F. OSMAN, MARK C. HIRONS, NOELLE C. KINYON, CHESTER S. OLSZEWSKI, KATIE R. LAMBERT, DAVID A. CARR
PHOTOGRAPHY CHRISTOPHER BARRETT
www.cannondesign.com

Clockwise from top:
A bold illuminated "thunderbolt" crosses the ceiling of the stylishly spare reception area. The feature starts at the elevator lobby, leading to the entry. Those seeking to decompress can do so in Alfredo Häberli lounges. The cool, calming hues of this glass hallway reappear elsewhere. Furnished with Konstantin Grcic Myoto chairs, the break room was designed to foster a sense of camaraderie. The bench-style trading stations.

4,200 sf
$90 per sf

DavidTan
Associates

ASSET MANAGEMENT FIRM, SINGAPORE

To lend a sense of home to a Swedish client's Singapore satellite office, DavidTan Associates design director Hoe Kiat Tan imported cool, Nordic style. Clean-lined furnishings were specified in pale woods, walls and floors are a sea of glossy white and warm gray, fuss is minimal. The Scandinavian aesthetic lends this asset management firm's digs a relaxed yet efficient feel.

Slabs of granite clad the entryway feature wall, adding texture to a scheme nearly free of ornamentation. Cement board animates meeting rooms and public zones. A cool palette of oak-veneer millwork and slate-hued carpet tiles give a nonchalant vibe to the two breakout areas.

The space originally had a very low ceiling, which the designer removed to reveal ample headroom—albeit crisscrossed with a maze of pipes. To maintain airiness while establishing a sense of order, Tan installed floating plaster ceiling elements that demarcate functional zones. In the entry, the plane is pierced with a strategically placed oval cutout; in the open-plan work area, the treatment is reversed, with oval canopies floating overhead like clouds. Boundaries are further drawn by glass walls that preserve brightness and spatial flow.

Workstations are super clean and spare, with quartets of high-tech Zefiro desks and Aeron chairs. Punctuating the minimalist environs are moments of visual pizzazz formed by wall panels wrapped in graphic textiles, including those of Midcentury Swedish design icon Josef Frank.

Clockwise from above: The waiting area is floored in agglomerated stone. In the larger conference room, business is conducted from mesh-back Eames Executive Office chairs. Near the entry, a pair of Gianluigi Landoni 1000 Fast armchairs lounge beneath a George Nelson Natural Ball clock. One of the smaller meeting rooms, furnished with Eames classics and a Bertjan Pot Random pendant. A breakout area, wrapped in oak veneer, is enlivened by Josef Frank's vibrant 1940s Aralia print. ➤

1 WAITING AREA

2 MEETING ROOM

3 BREAKOUT AREA

4 OPEN OFFICE

5 PANTRY AND UTILITY

The ceiling in the open-plan workspace is the inverse of that in the public areas. Below fluorescent lights, double rows of workstations are separated by glass panels.

PROJECT TEAM HOE KIAT (DAVID) TAN, VERONICA HO
PHOTOGRAPHY CHAN
www.davidtan.com.sg

Arcturis

EDWARD JONES TRAINING FACILITY, ST. LOUIS

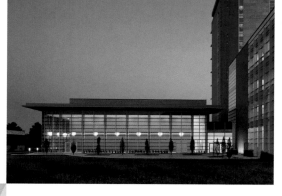

380,000 sf
New construction

Clockwise from above: A diversity of meeting and lounge spaces support the various training levels offered. Zinc, limestone, and terracotta were used on the exterior, as were solar louvers. Custom pendants line a hall flooded with natural light; on the terracotta wall is a company watchword. Pre-function spaces open to an exterior courtyard. The cafeteria offers seating of several kinds, and outdoor dining is also an option. Stairs linking the first through third floors add informal meeting space via landings.

Edward Jones takes pride in a culture of "connection, collaboration, and inspiration," and this massive new facility shows it walks the walk. Known for a personalized approach in guiding clients toward wise investments, the company invests as wisely in its people and their work environment. A top priority is attracting new talent and training associates—the firm's financial advisors serve nearly 7 million investors in North America alone.

A goal was for the building to have a transparent feel, highlighting the movement of people inside and inviting the outdoors in. Thus, Arcturis made the "spine" of operations a four-story glass atrium, with main program elements branching to either side. Four floors of the structure are reserved for training over 1,400 people; office space on five upper levels accommodates 700 associates.

The cafeteria, overlooking a pleasant green courtyard, can handle some 500 people at lunch—at once. That number grows for training and business presentations thanks to a seating system that retracts under the stage and within a wall cavity. Operable partitions accommodate several different room configurations.

Energy efficiency is of great concern: The building's north-south orientation maximizes natural-daylight opportunities, and solar power is tapped as well. And though future performance is famously hard to predict, the outlook is sunny indeed.

PHOTOGRAPHY DAVE BURK/HEDRICH BLESSING
www.arcturis.com

GKV Architects

FINANCIAL INSTITUTION
NEW YORK

Clockwise from right: In reception, gears salvaged from a Hudson Valley paper mill symbolize collaborative effort; seating is by Tanju Özelgin. Photomurals line corridors whose canted oak-veneer canopies direct light. Open-concept workstations by Allsteel abet the flow of daylight and foster collaboration. Near the waiting area, artist Pete De Mattia's sheet metal–and–crystal "teleidescope" (part telescope, part kaleidoscope) has the Woolworth Building in its sights. A conference room enjoys spectacular 360-degree views. ➤

Hired to design a financial client's 7 World Trade Center space, GKV delivered a sophisticated, ecofriendly interior that capitalizes on natural illumination and 360-degree views—on a tight budget, no less. The architects did so by playing against corporate-office convention, flip-flopping the typical layout. The plan pushes workstations, conference rooms, and a café to prime perimeter real estate and positions glass-walled individual offices at the building's core in order to maximize daylight penetration.

This more egalitarian configuration encourages the culture of interaction, collaboration, and creativity that the client aspired to. The three floors the company occupies are stitched together by an ornamental stair that further reinforces the notion of connectivity while also reducing elevator usage and thus energy costs.

From the project's inception, the art program was an important component. More than 170 pieces from the client's private collection of modern and contemporary works are displayed throughout the office, with many livening the corridors.

By exploiting sunlight, controlling air quality, salvaging materials, eliminating waste, and incorporating products made from recycled materials, the project achieved LEED Platinum status—and kudos from the client.

160,000 sf
LEED Platinum

1 RECEPTION

2 CONFERENCE ROOM

3 TRADING FLOOR

4 CAFÉ

5 BREAKOUT AREA

6 WORKSTATIONS

7 PRIVATE OFFICE

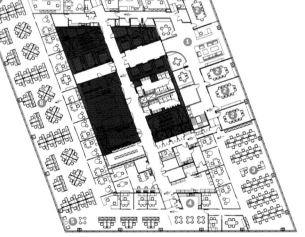

Clockwise from opposite top: Library-print wall covering by Atelier Abigail Ahern brings sophistication and whimsy to a quiet work area. A view through De Mattia's teleidoscope. Doors to conference rooms are oak veneer. A conference room has prime corner real estate. Stained-oak veneer animates executive workstations. The café/conference area features tables and chairs by Harter.

PROJECT TEAM RANDOLPH GERNER, BRYAN BENNETT, JUTTA ISHII, JULIA MEIER
PHOTOGRAPHY ERIC LAIGNEL
www.gkvarchitects.com

Rapt Studio

RCM CAPITAL MANAGEMENT, SAN FRANCISCO

For its new offices in the city's financial district, RCM presented Rapt Studio with a hefty challenge. The designers would have 120 days to come up with a solution—and be ready for move-in, too. RCM wanted to make significant changes to its current office atmosphere, focusing on an open environment that would nurture collaboration and showcase its forward-thinking attitude. In addition, the firm planned to pursue LEED certification as part of its global sustainability initiative.

Initially, Rapt met with the client every other day, employing structured working sessions and clear goal setting to facilitate rapid decision-making during the schedule's most aggressive period. The budget was appropriate but not extravagant, so Rapt needed to deliver maximum impact for the best value. Using a spare vocabulary of concrete flooring, alternating pendant and recessed lights, clean-lined but comfortable furniture, and abundant glass, Rapt created a space at once pared-back and approachable. Seating is modern but inviting, with auxiliary pieces—coffee tables, hanging lamps, café chairs—that would work equally well in a residential setting.

Four months later: Mission accomplished. Oh, and the project was certified LEED Silver.

Clockwise from right: A steel-and-glass staircase links the upper-level reception and lower-level waiting areas; Martin Battrud lounge chairs, a Noguchi coffee table, and concrete flooring lend panache. Artwork stands in for a view on the conference room's interior wall. A river-stone pathway courses beneath the stairs. Frameless glazing by Million Glass gives a private office an airy vibe. The SF Millwork wood-veneer ceiling meets Golden Gate graphics in reception. ➤

35,000 sf
LEED Silver

PROJECT TEAM JAMES POLLET, CHRISTINE SHAW, NATHANIEL HAYNES, LYDIA CHAN
GENERAL CONTRACTOR SKYLINE CONSTRUCTION
MEP ENGINEER WPS-FLACK & KURTZ
STRUCTURAL ENGINEER MIDDLEBROOK AND LOUIE
FURNITURE MANUFACTURER HERMAN MILLER
FURNITURE DEALER CRI
AUDIOVISUAL CONSULTANT ANDERSON A/V

PHOTOGRAPHY ERIC LAIGNEL

www.raptstudio.com

Clockwise from above: Louis Poulsen PH5 pendants alternate with Delray Swing fixtures in the conference room. Glass balustrades make the stairwell feel expansive. An open-backed credenza in a private office helps put the emphasis on the view. Eames Wire chairs with red leather seat pads offer a punch of color in the café.

Desai/Chia Architecture

KEFFI GROUP, NEW YORK

Employees of this boutique investment and venture-capital firm have their heads in the clouds—almost literally. The office, located on the 44th floor of a high-rise near Bryant Park, has stellar views of both sky and skyline. Desai/Chia's evanescent design keeps the emphasis on the panorama by dematerializing interior walls: All rooms are enclosed in planes of glass that slip directly into the floor and ceiling, without obvious framing, to appear nearly invisible.

Such visual and spatial openness suits Keffi Group's collaborative working style to a T. There are no private offices; instead, employees share generously sized workstations surfaced in milky-white resin. Glass-box conference rooms and informal "think tanks" for casual brainstorming are interspersed throughout the floorplan, creating subtle separation between zones while enhancing acoustic privacy. Bubinga-veneer casegoods serve as a foil to the pale finishes, injecting warmth and texture; so do elaborate carved-stone *jali* screens, a feature derived from Indian palace architecture.

Like the office itself, the 16-foot-long conference table appears to float in midair. The piece, whose top is held aloft by just two slim plinths, was custom designed in collaboration with structural engineering firm Arup. As with the ethereal decor, the table is more hardworking than it first appears: A concealed wiring trough and flip-up grommets provide full IT and AV connectivity.

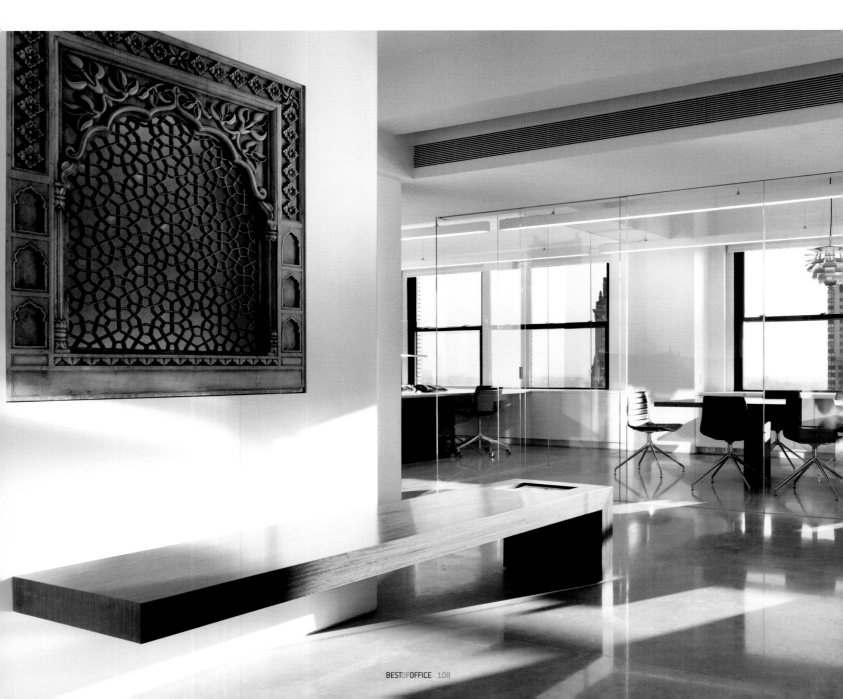

Clockwise from left:
Above reception's bubinga bench is an LED-backlit carved-stone jali, one of several that the client requested be incorporated into the design. Reinforcing spatial continuity, linear fixtures by Zumtobel express a consistent line of light throughout the open-plan office; bronze Louis Poulsen Artichoke lamps cast an inviting glow. The conference rooms' glass walls—sans visible framing— recess into troughs in the floor and ceiling, creating a sense of boundarylessness. ➤

One of the two acoustically private "think tanks," furnished with felt-covered Paola Lenti Aladdin lounges; the floors throughout are honed travertine slabs. ➤

Clockwise from left: *In the library, a traditional hand-carved stone arch from India adorns an illuminated niche above bubinga-veneer shelves. Both bathrooms are clad in travertine; faucet controls are mounted to the front of the cantilever counter for easy access. Like the other meeting spaces, the 14-seat main conference room is sheathed in a glass skin that maintains acoustic privacy while offering views into adjacent work areas; Catifa chairs by Arper are upholstered in Spinneybeck leather.*

4,000 sf
Renovation

1 RECEPTION
2 CONFERENCE ROOM
3 MEETING ROOM
4 THINK TANK
5 LIBRARY
6 WORKSTATIONS

PROJECT TEAM KATHERINE CHIA, ARJUN DESAI
STRUCTURAL ENGINEER ARUP
MEP ENGINEER EDWARDS & ZUCK
LIGHTING CONSULTANT CHRISTINE SCIULLI LIGHT + DESIGN
CONSTRUCTION MANAGER RICHTER+RATNER
PHOTOGRAPHY PAUL WARCHOL
www.desaichia.com

"The glass walls disappear from view, creating a visual continuity that promotes group work and a sense of collective engagement"
—KATHERINE CHIA

IA Interior
Architects

MESIROW FINANCIAL HEADQUARTERS, CHICAGO

348,000 rentable sf
LEED Gold

*Clockwise from
above: In reception,
Rodolfo Dordoni floor
lamps flank leather
chairs. The reception
desk is composed of
backlit resin, back-
painted glass, and
a block of marble.
Glazed curtain walls
flood reception with
light. Zebrawood
panels mark the
entrance to an "oasis"
area housing a
pantry, small
conference room,
and copy center.
A Foscarini Big Bang
pendant adds energy
to an oasis with
Coalesse and Davis
furnishings. Custom
pendants from Boyd
Lighting and a
polycarbonate faux
skylight crown an
elevator lobby.* ➤

In 1937, FDR led the nation, Amelia Earhart disappeared over the Pacific Ocean, and financial-services firm Mesirow Financial was founded. IA Interior Architects masterminded the venerable company's first-ever move, consolidating multiple locations in a world headquarters spread over 12 floors of a downtown high-rise. The brief was to honor the client's entrepreneurial spirit and successful history while embracing its future.

To guide the design, IA used a web-based survey that gathered data from over 750 Mesirow staffers and 28 department leaders. The consensus? That the space needed to accommodate teaming activities and one-on-one client meetings in equal measure. Thus a balance of workstations and glass-front private offices sited to take advantage of daylight pouring in through full-height windows. Moreover, the facility is almost entirely modular; a flexible planning grid placed infrastructure above the ceiling plane to enable endless reconfigurations. It is also ecofriendly: LEED Gold was achieved via occupancy- and daylight-harvesting sensors, energy-efficient light fixtures, and Green Glance software that manages energy consumption on a floor-by-floor basis.

Throughout, contemporary and traditional elements intermingle. The reception desk, for instance, features a transaction top of Calacatta marble set into a frame of backlit citron resin. On a nearby wall hangs a sawtooth custom artwork by Kahler Slater that, like a lenticular, changes depending on your vantage. Seen from one direction, it speaks to the company's roots with an aerial view of Chicago; from the other, a perspective map of the world signifies the firm's global reach.

PROJECT TEAM TOM POWERS, ARTURO FEBRY, RICHELLE ALLEN, R.J. BRENNAN, ANN MARIE KROL, CARRIE HANN, MATT LANO, KEVIN PORTER

PHOTOGRAPHY CHRISTOPHER BARRETT

www.interiorarchitects.com

Clockwise from above: A wide perimeter corridor houses a pair of Roger Persson Happy chairs and a Barbara Barry Oval Egg coffee table; city views are shared with a glass-front conference room. An office area boasts Steelcase workstations and KI demountable walls. A typical oasis lounge, with Coalesse Bob chairs and Denizen personal tables.

1 ELEVATOR LOBBY

2 WORKSTATIONS

3 OFFICE

4 MEETING ROOM

5 OASIS LOUNGE

0   10   20   40

Ted Moudis Associates

TRADING FIRM, NEW YORK

This project proves the trope "Every picture tells a story," alas, accurate. The client sought an established yet progressive aesthetic for its New York headquarters. The decor would telegraph the firm's past, present, and future by integrating design elements honoring its traditional roots with those nodding to its forward-looking ethos.

Ted Moudis Associates delivered the established via its use of patterned stone floors, coffered ceilings, detailed wall bases, and crown molding in the more formal areas, lending a strong sense of "refined comfort." On the progressive side are the more modern employee areas, with intensified tones and residential details conducive to decompressing. The CEO's favorite color—blue—unites the spaces.

Sight lines were of utmost importance, as was flexibility within the open-office environment. The design team had to consider the visual connections on the trading floor as well as those between traders and private offices. They worked with Innovant to develop furniture that, with slight modifications, allows an administrative workstation to function as a trading desk and vice versa. Such adaptability facilitates expansion and other possible migrations.

Tranquil surroundings, catered lunches in a comfortable lounge/dining area, a gym with lockers and showers: Everything in this picture feels just right.

Clockwise from left:
In the elevator lobby, bronze pendants with alabaster shades hang from a simple coffered ceiling; the double-glass doors leading to reception are framed in bronze. Ball-chain curtains surround the circular "green room." Private offices are fronted in wood-framed glass. A large warming kitchen supports daily catered buffet lunches at the well-stocked café. The breakout lounge, one café-seating option. The half-inch bronze banding pattern of reception's marble flooring commences at the elevators.

61,500 sf

PROJECT TEAM TED MOUDIS, CHRISTOPHER SAVOGLOU, PERRY LUONGO,
JOHN FERRANTE, JACQUELINE BARR, MICHAEL SINKEW, KIMBERLY SHARPE
PHOTOGRAPHY ADRIAN WILSON
www.tedmoudis.com

BT Arquitectos

BRESLAU CAPITAL, PUNTA PAITILLA, PANAMA

Clockwise from below: *A raised floor and illuminated ceiling give the spare administrative zone a futuristic mien; rich oak woodwork provides a warm foil to the glossy surfaces. The frosted glass louvers measure 8 inches wide. A view from the conference room into the reception and waiting areas.* ➤

In the context of modern office design, glass walls are frequently employed to instill openness and symbolize corporate transparency. But for this financial firm's Panama location, BT Arquitectos wanted to utilize glass in an unexpected and compelling manner, to create spaces that could be as visible or private as desired.

The solution was to enclose rooms in clear tempered glazing backed with vertical slats of frosted glass. Oriented perpendicularly to the walls, the frosted fins create the effect of a louvered screen, obscuring the inward view from an oblique angle. Most of the offices, including those of the CEO and CFO, receive this double-layer treatment.

A savvy floorplan enhances the sense of privacy. All spaces flow around a central lounge—dubbed the chill-out room—that's enclosed in solid walls. Its white-oak cladding answered the client's request for a modern scheme, which presents as confident, rich, and elegant. Subtly mismatched in hue, the woodwork offers a warm base for the other elements to play off of. Furnishings are clean-lined, primarily black and white, in unusually sumptuous fabrics and leather. Warm lighting lends the space greater intimacy—and a feel more boutique hotel than investment firm.

1 RECEPTION
2 DECOMPRESSION ZONE
3 CHILL-OUT ROOM
4 CONFERENCE ROOM
5 CFO'S OFFICE
6 CEO'S OFFICE
7 PRIVATE OFFICE
8 ADMINISTRATION

0   10   20   40

2,400 sf
$350,000 budget

PROJECT TEAM TEOFILO TARAZI, ALEXANDER CHI
PHOTOGRAPHY JAIME JUSTINIANI
www.bt.com.pa

Clockwise from opposite: Located at the center of the floor plate, the oak-lined chill-out room is the only (nearly) fully enclosed space; its suite of leather seating is brightened by a Moooi Random pendant. Visible from reception, the chill-out room seems to float on its frosted glass base. The conference room, as seen through its louvered wall. The CFO's office is an island unto itself yet remains visually accessible.

Lindsay Newman Architecture and Design

JLL PARTNERS, NEW YORK

Imagine being in the offices of a leveraged buyout–and–private equity investment firm, about to negotiate the riskiest deal of your life. Discounting a tropical desert island, what sort of space would most calm your jangled nerves?

This was the question Cat Lindsay set out to answer when JLL Partners hired her to mastermind its new space. At the first office she designed for the company—in 1994, on the 33rd floor of the same Lexington Avenue building—Lindsay captured natural light and sweeping city views to Zen-like effect. This time, two flights down, the challenge was to create a state-of-the-art conference room and reception area where clients could unwind before a meeting.

Lindsay configured the layout to be as capacious as possible. Private offices equipped with French doors and sidelights span the perimeter, offering privacy and coaxing in sunshine. At the center of the floor plate are bullpens punctuated by modular clusters of desks, designed to accommodate two- and four-person teams.

In keeping with the feng shui–inspired floorplan, the lighting scheme was conceived to evoke calm. In lieu of an acoustic ceiling with recessed cans, lay lights filtered through an acrylic lens brighten the space. Downlights, meanwhile, set work surfaces aglow.

The final touch, the palette, is a soothing combination of sage-green carpet, Anigre millwork, and leather upholstery, all of which put clients at ease in a setting at once modern and soft—even when they're on deck.

Clockwise from above: The architects designed the coffee tables and leather-front reception desk. A private restroom adjacent to the conference area. The welcoming reception, as seen from the elevator lobby. The view from the private dining room to the boardroom reveals Vitra chairs and a custom table by Paul Downs.

21,000 sf
Renovation

DESIGN PRINCIPAL CAT LINDSAY

PHOTOGRAPHY CHRIS COOPER

lnarchitecture.com

0 10 20   40

1 RECEPTION

2 BOARDROOM

3 PRIVATE DINING

4 MEETING ROOM

5 LUNCHROOM

6 PRIVATE OFFICES

7 BULLPENS

24,575 sf
Adaptive reuse

Box Studios

MEGASTAR FINANCIAL, DENVER

Needing a new headquarters, MegaStar Financial purchased a former dairy building and brought Box Studios on board for a major renovation. The design team's goal was to incorporate natural light throughout by envisioning a massive clerestory and atrium at the heart of the structure. The feature sent natural light flooding down into a windowless basement, doubling the office's usable square footage in the process—and instantly increasing the value of the property.

The only catch? "Having to cut a 20-by-20-foot opening into the roof in the middle of a snowy Colorado winter," firm principal Lynn Coit recalls. It was an especially tricky move given that the roof was made of cast concrete and that Box Studios was straining to avoid adding structural columns. But for all its engineering challenges, the atrium is a stunning visual centerpiece—complete with a dramatic installation of floating pendant lights—for a space that was once plagued with choppy interior walls, oppressively low soffits, and an overarching sense of darkness.

Another contribution to the building's new demeanor is the vivid primary-yellow palette. Against a background of white Interlam-clad walls and charcoal carpeting are vibrant pops of citrus hues. The café is especially playful: A translucent yellow-and-white polka-dot wall serves as its backdrop. Yet the architects carefully implemented the flashier touches only in modular ways, using removable panels that could be swapped out down the line, for instance. After all, the building is now one that MegaStar could occupy for a very, very long time. "The materials can be reinterpreted," says Coit. "But the architecture is timeless."

Clockwise from above: An accent wall of gloss-white sculptured panels by Interlam is a textural counterpoint to the sleek surfaces of the reception desk. In the employee café, naturally backlit Lumicor resin panels form a lively backdrop to the Corian Internet bar. New clerestory windows cut into the roof cast light through the glass-rail main staircase and into the basement. A carbon-fiber and glass pendant arrangement by Vibia spotlights a chunky block of Corian. Paper-thin wood-veneer lights cascade down the main atrium.

PROJECT TEAM CATHY LOFTUS, LYNN COIT, JIM GRACZYK, KAYE MULLANEY, BRIE BANE
PHOTOGRAPHY RON JOHNSON
www.bxstudios.com

Gary Lee Partners

THE BOSTON CONSULTING GROUP, CHICAGO

It was only natural that BCG would tap Gary Lee Partners to design its Chicago office: The two firms have a long history of creative partnership. Moving to a new downtown space, BCG wanted to retain the sophisticated character of its previous home—also by Gary Lee—while fitting the same number of employees into less overall square footage. The challenge was to establish standards that minimize real estate and anticipate future growth...without sacrificing a sense of personal space.

Modifications were made to the building core, including a new staircase and fire grill that links all five BCG floors and provides a strong unifying element. Meeting and lounge spaces are interspersed throughout; many can be expanded or reconfigured as needed to accommodate large or small gatherings. Connectivity between teaming and work areas creates a collaborative vibe.

The taut, efficient office feels airy courtesy of floor-to-ceiling glass partitions standing in for solid walls, ensuring that daylight penetrates interior areas. Although the look is modern, with clean lines and little in the way of decoration, warm woods, luxurious textiles, and polished stone lend warmth. And grouped around the perimeter are low-slung sofas and tables where two people can enjoy a more focused interaction—or simply recharge while taking in the spectacular view.

Clockwise from above: Custom chairs in reception were designed by Gary Lee; the Ion coffee table is from Chai Ming Studios, the design firm's furniture line. Private offices feel larger than they are thanks to spare furnishings and full-height glass; door panels display the occupant's name and personal photo. Reception's louvered Tamo divider creates separation but allows light to flow. ➤

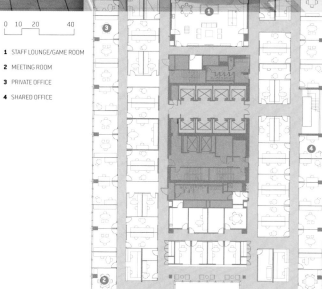

0 10 20   40

1 STAFF LOUNGE/GAME ROOM

2 MEETING ROOM

3 PRIVATE OFFICE

4 SHARED OFFICE

Clockwise from above: *A multiuse area, complete with pantry, is easy to reconfigure. Abundant glass keeps corridors bright. The millwork louvers in reception screen the waiting area. Teaming spaces, such as this conversation spot with Viccarbe tables and chairs, are grouped on window walls. Glazed partitions make smaller offices feel expansive. A break area is anchored by Chilewich flooring.*

PROJECT TEAM GARY LEE, DAVID GROUT, DANA KOCH, MAURA O'MAHONEY, TIM SALISBURY

PHOTOGRAPHY STEVE HALL/HEDRICH BLESSING (1–3, 5–8), NATHAN KIRKMAN (4)

www.garyleepartners.com

creative

Designers designing design digs?

Try saying that three times fast! The process often proves as tricky as the pronunciation.

That's because industry professionals demand limber spaces that nourish solo work and cross-pollination in equal measure and double as a tool for wooing and inspiring clients. Hence designers getting creative with their work spaces, putting them to use as event venues, galleries, and product showrooms, too: A great way to add value and intrigue. *And to walk the talk.*

5,000 sf
$25 per sf

CL3 Architects Limited

CL3 STUDIO, HONG KONG

Clockwise from above: *Epoxy flooring, an exposed waffle ceiling dotted with energy-efficient bulbs, and a reception desk of plywood and sheet metal announce the industrial aesthetic. Metal gates secure the office at night. A quiet room at rear offers a spot for Skype chats and small group meetings. With workstations set along the window wall, employees enjoy daylight and panoramic views of Hong Kong. CL3 Studio clients are invariably impressed with the firm's creative cost-cutting measures, such as the joint Ping-Pong/ conference table.*

Is it *more* or *less* challenging for architects to design their own offices than others'? For CL3, building out its Hong Kong studio proved a bit of both. The difficulty was that the firm couldn't devote as much time to the project as it would have for a proper client. The easy part? That managing director William Lim could make all the decisions himself.

Other than maximizing the meager budget, a top priority was to be as environmentally responsible as possible. The design team achieved those aims by blending new construction with recycled furnishings and materials and by adhering to a spare, industrial aesthetic. Cost-effective solutions included raw plywood millwork, the reuse of system furniture from CL3's previous office, and a sliding metal gate that secures the space at night (and lends an edgy touch during working hours). Curtains delineate the triangular floor plate in lieu of solid partitions, and work spaces are set along the window wall to take advantage of daylight.

Lim notes that the best part of the office might well be the conference room's Ping-Pong table: Between sets, it seats 12 for meetings.

MANAGING DIRECTOR WILLIAM LIM
PHOTOGRAPHER NIRUT BENJABANPOT/CL3
www.cl3.com

After 15 years based in a former tobacco warehouse, Arcturis was ready to move on. Taking such a step was, as one might expect, easier said than done. How does a design studio go about envisioning its own space—no less a creative test lab—without succumbing to perfectionism or being overcome by the unending possibilities?

The firm tackled the job systematically and innovatively, with minimum angst and maximum smarts. First, a client team and a design team were established; second, objectives such as sustainability, flexibility, and collaboration were defined; third, a space compatible with these goals was chosen: the second floor of a downtown high-rise.

Next, the firm organized a Saturday charette focusing on key program elements—arrival/meeting space, individual/team work areas, production area, break area, and library—and netted some solutions, like the

brainstorming room. It also yielded eco-conscious ideas like showers for bike riders, the use of local materials, and discounts on public transportation.

The plans ended up including multiple types of conference rooms: Some support presentations, learning, and meetings; others support collaboration, socializing, and quiet relaxation. Large pin-up panels and multiple flatscreens communicate the firm's scope to visitors. The office is everything a designer could ever want, because who knows better than designers themselves?

Arcturis

ARCTURIS OFFICE, ST. LOUIS

30,000 sf
LEED Silver

From opposite top:
In reception and throughout, existing concrete floors and beams were cleaned and polished, creating a rustic, mottled effect. Full-length windows provide some 90 percent of the staff with city views and natural light from their desks, benefits shown to reduce stress and enhance productivity. One of the many informal breakout areas. The waffle-grid ceiling, made with poured concrete, was painted white. Many products utilize regional materials, like the ultracool (also concrete) restroom trough sink, created in St. Louis by CK Design.

PHOTOGRAPHY DEBBIE FRANKE

www.arcturis.com

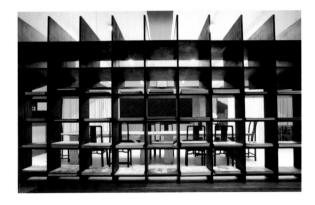

PLATFORM (1X2), HONG KONG

CL3 Architects Limited and OpenUU

This edgy warehouse was built to multitask. By day, it performs double duty as the studio of the design research lab OpenUU and a gallery exhibiting the art collection of CL3 managing director William Lim. At night, it's a venue for entertaining the city's culturati.

The key to flexibility is a massive three-dimensional grid—dubbed Platform (1x2)—that serves as a library, storage unit, video-viewing stage, and spatial divider. The boxy structure was built from 40-by-79-inch (or 1-by-2-meter, hence the name) plywood modules assembled entirely without nails; tongue-and-groove joints hold everything firmly in place. "The piece injects character and functionality while preserving the desirable rawness of an abandoned building," explain OpenUU managing director Kevin Lim and creative director Edward Kim. "The project was carefully orchestrated to highlight the benefits of adaptive reuse and minimizing waste."

To maintain that raw aesthetic, existing columns and walls were left exposed. Furniture was salvaged from nearby secondhand markets or made with recycled content. LED lighting saves energy. Doors opening to a terrace allow for natural ventilation—or, during evening events, for fresh air. Indeed, when cocktail and dinner parties are held, the platform takes on yet another role: major conversation piece.

Clockwise from above: The plywood grid measures 26 by 40 feet; visible beyond is the studio work table. An adjacent sitting area features salvaged furniture and a custom pushcart coffee table. Stowaway space, accessed via hydraulic-hinged doors, is hidden in the platform base. The gallery occupies a sizable portion of the interior. ➤

PROJECT TEAM CL3: WILLIAM LIM.
OPENUU: KEVIN LIM, EDDY KIM, EDWARD KIM
ENGINEER OPENUU
PHOTOGRAPHY NIRUT BENJABANPOT/CL3
www.cl3.com
www.openuu.com

1 ENTRY
2 PANTRY
3 STUDIO/TABLE
4 TERRACE
5 SITTING AREA
6 PLATFORM
7 VIDEO PROJECTION WALL
8 GALLERY
9 RESTROOM

0   10   20   40

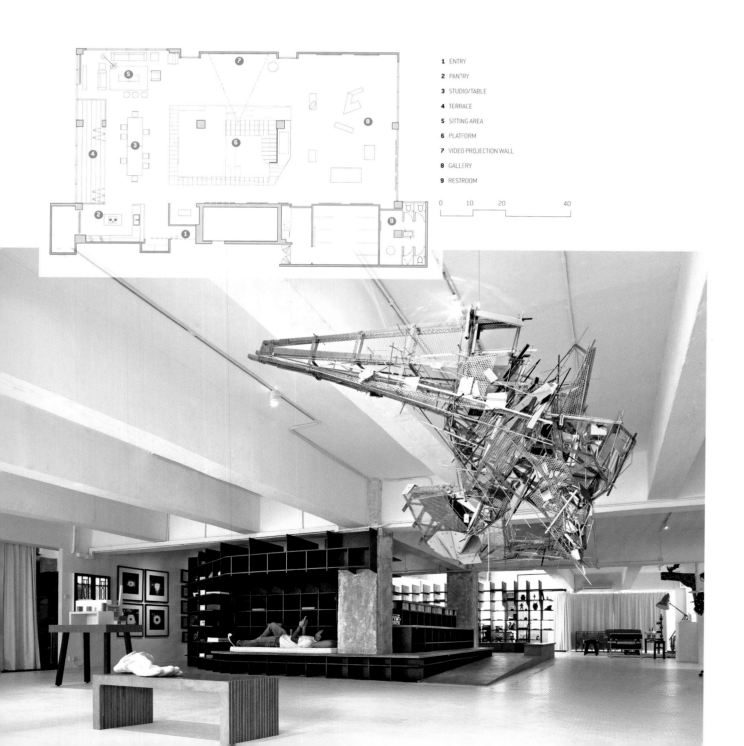

Clockwise from above: The platform's integrated seating includes bleacher-style benches—and even a mattress for relaxing. Made of scrap plywood, the studio work surface becomes a dining table for after-hour events; doors at the right open onto a terrace with mountain views. An exercise in frugality and waste reduction, the pantry was purchased as a floor sample from a nearby kitchen showroom. The platform floats in the floor plate's center, separating gallery, studio, and video-viewing areas. The rough-concrete and exposed-stone walls of the unisex restroom contrast smartly with the sleek fixtures and glossy tiles.

It's important to practice what you preach, and that's what this global interiors firm has done in its New York regional office. Employing the kind of advice the firm typically presents to clients, the design team devised a space reflecting a workplace philosophy that invites staff interaction and client collaboration. In opting for modest, efficient, and open personal areas as opposed to large private cubicles, the team delivered a layout designed to encourage co-workers to meet and engage.

The most dramatic example is in the library, coffee bar, and pantry work areas, which merge into one visual and functional centerpiece. The Teammate Café, as it's known, is the most highly trafficked area for activity and intermingling. Elements include pared-down shelving for catalogs and touchable samples; an oversize island conducive to designer meetings; and a motorized front screen and projector for presentations. Although the entire space is open to the reception area—to accommodate larger gatherings—a full curtain can be drawn for more intimate pow-wows. Use of benching in the work area provides more staffing space, as well as hoteling stations for virtual workers and visitors.

The results support a culture in which the collaborative nature of design is sustained by the work environment.

Nelson

NELSON OFFICE, NEW YORK

Clockwise from opposite: *The Teammate Café, the heart of the office, opens to reception, allowing for diverse gatherings. A corrugated ceiling treatment defines the main path through the office while concealing ductwork. Transom glass is flush with brightly colored walls, keeping the space light-filled and expansive. Modest personal cubes foster collaboration and productivity. A sinuous wall draws visitors from entry to reception.*

PROJECT TEAM JOHN NELSON, BOB KELLNER, JONATHAN NICHOLS
PHOTOGRAPHY HALKIN PHOTOGRAPHY
www.nelsononline.com

10,000 sf
Renovation

Ezequielfarca

EZEQUIELFARCA DESIGN STUDIO AND SHOWROOM, MEXICO CITY

At the Ezequielfarca showroom in the Polanco district, furnishings from the designer/manufacturer's own label and those of other brands it represents share a common aesthetic. Clean, contemporary lines and a harmonizing mix of natural materials prevail. A conference table, for example, tops an iron base with biomorphic resin top. In the black-painted reception nook, a wood-covered pendant hangs above a timber-clad check-in desk. If this bi-level space is the realized vision of chief creative director/CEO Ezequiel Farca, then the firm's design studio, on the building's third floor, is the genesis; the interplay of textures emulates his philosophy of integrated design.

At the entry to the loftlike studio, a slatted floor-to-ceiling vertical screen allows for the passage of light and air. Opposite, a glass wall overlooking a terrace coaxes in a generous dose of daylight. Two long white-lacquered desks, their linearity reinforced by attenuated Corian pendants, provide room for a dozen designers—interior, industrial, and graphic—to collaborate. Not only is the studio itself open but the culture is, too: The firm's residential and commercial clients are invited to review concepts as they're being developed.

The three floors are connected by a marble stair enclosed in chalkboard-painted walls, which staffers flourish with an ever changing rotation of off-the-cuff sketches and musings. As with the firm's work, it's all about the hand finishes.

From top: Furnishings by Ezequielfarca and other lines that the showroom represents are displayed on faux-wood laminate flooring. Near the reception, curve-back wire-frame armchairs and a freeform conference table offset the rectilinear architecture. ➤

Clockwise from left: In the third-floor studio, a slatted MDF privacy screen allows the flow of air into the stairwell; the Corian light fixture is by Ezequielfarca. The street-level façade. A straight-run marble staircase leads from the ground level to the showroom's second story and the third-floor studio. Reflecting the firm's open culture, Farca shares work space with the staff. A wall of metal shelving houses books, magazines, and materials. A dining vignette on the showroom's second floor. Furniture models in the studio. Reception's cheeky signage. Stairwell walls are coated with acrylic-based chalkboard paint.

PHOTOGRAPHY JAIME NARARRO

www.ezequielfarca.com

1 STAIRCASE

2 WORKSTATIONS

3 CEO'S DESK

4 PRIVATE OFFICE

5 TERRACE

0   5   10   20

1,270 sf
3 stories

YOU (YES, YOU)

design/manufacturing

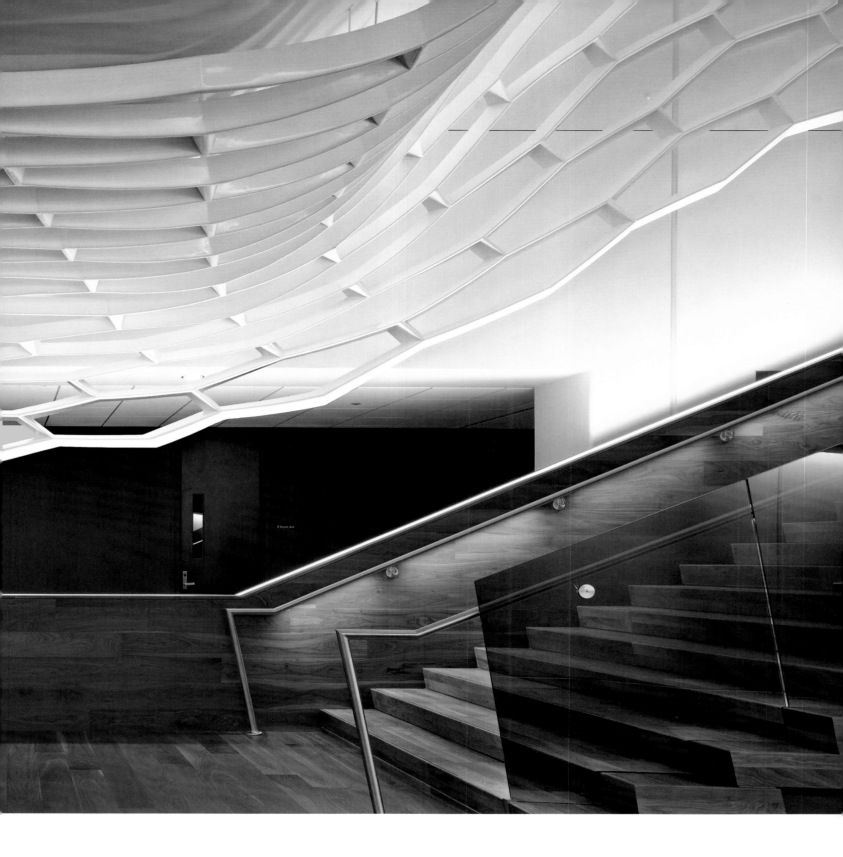

Where do product manufacturers
find office-decor inspiration? In the very products they design and fabricate,
of course. Which in this case includes contract
furniture, commercial carpets, home furnishings, and high-performance fibers—all building blocks of contemporary interiors.
These companies are innovators, and their work spaces reflect the ingenuity and ideation they traffic in. Each office proves a
canny hybrid of think tank, fab shop, showroom, and entertainment venue. *Who's inspired now?*

Shimoda Design Group and Steelcase Design

STEELCASE WORK CAFÉ
GRAND RAPIDS, MICHIGAN

Potted ferns and grow lights included, the Steelcase cafeteria had remained untouched since 1983. Tapped to mastermind a thorough overhaul, Joey Shimoda envisioned more than just a stylish spot for employees to grab lunch. He embraced the client's mandate to be sensitive to new directions in workplace innovation—in this case, the concept of the nomadic employee.

An experimental hybrid, the Work Café is a cafeteria with an office program. A concierge desk sits at the bottom of a grand staircase, which descends from the main lobby to the below-grade eatery. In addition to directing guests to one of five meeting rooms, the concierge can suggest a private phone booth or a quiet room for waiting.

Tucked beneath the stairs is a welcome center equipped with video monitors that feature updates on corporate events. Those awaiting colleagues naturally migrate to the coffee bar, where a bank of screens gives an overview of company goings-on. A pair of angular counter-height tables with barstools offers communal seating, multiplying opportunities for people to meet and talk.

The route to the dining room leads through the "art forest," a grove of slim stainless-steel pillars, each engraved with company patent numbers (employees can find products they helped design). Seating in the expansive lounge is by Steelcase, of course, creating what Shimoda calls "a palette of postures": Stand, sit, perch, or lounge as you eat or work.

1 COFFEE BAR

2 BUSINESS CENTER

3 LOUNGE

4 MEEETING ROOMS

5 ART FOREST

6 DINING AREA

7 STUDY

8 KITCHEN

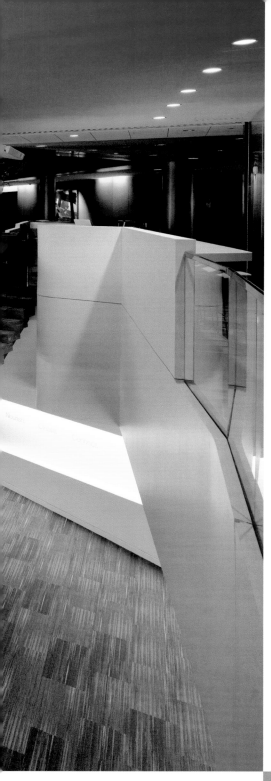

Clockwise from far left: The canopy, which extends 80 feet, is supported by painted steel cables. Walnut veneer clads the exterior of a pair of meeting rooms. In the dining room, chairs with polypropylene seats surround tables by Josep Llusca. Full-height windows coax sunlight into the lounge. ➤

Clockwise from above: Outdoor seating cozies up to a fire pit. In the lounge, chairs by Brian Kane surround a William Sorel table. Between the servery and the dining room, stainless-steel "trees" rise 12 feet to the mirrored ceiling. Cove lighting defines the lounge, furnished with sofas by Eoos; in the adjacent coffee bar, stools by Patricia Urquiola line two counter-height tables. A welcome area is tucked under the staircase.

PROJECT TEAM SUSAN CHANG, JOEY SHIMODA, DANIEL ALLEN, TODD TUNTLAND, DAVID KHUONG, BENJAMIN GROBE, YING-LING SUN, ANDRE KRAUSE, ELIZABETH CAO

PHOTOGRAPHY BENNY CHAN/FOTOWORKS

www.shimodadesign.com

Kellie Smith
Design Studio

SWISSTEX AMERICA, DALTON, GEORGIA

PROJECT TEAM KELLIE SMITH, JEROME HOLLIS
PHOTOGRAPHY MELANIE SUGGS
www.kelliesmithdesignstudio.com

Clockwise from above: Glass walls give the project an airy feel, especially in the CEO's snug office, which is less than 10 feet wide. A custom stainless-steel staircase may be the focal point of the design, but details like a Melanie Hönig lightbulb painting speak to the founders' passion for art. An Ashley Kinnamon mural hangs behind the desk of the CEO. A Paul Fontana fiber painting resides in the lobby, designed to be both sophisticated and inviting. In the break room, antique chairs were painted to match a series of yellow safety markings on the steps. Smith flipped the main staircase 90 degrees from its former orientation, a bold move that increased usable space in the lobby.

It makes perfect sense that the U.S. representative of a multinational textile company would be headquartered in tiny Dalton, Georgia, population 33,000. Nicknamed the Carpet Capital of the World, the town is home to some 150 plants that produce the vast majority of the planet's commercial carpeting supply. Far less obvious, when SwissTex took over a dilapidated building on a busy corner, was how to visually reconcile the brand's new small-town industrial quarters with its big-city European roots.

Kellie Smith rebuilt the space—actually an ad hoc assemblage of three boxy warehouses—using glass walls to open the dark and cramped offices. She then referenced area history with an industrial-modern motif, deploying a cool, neutral palette and commissioning a local business to make a staircase of stainless steel and concrete. The design scheme needed to sit well with those working on-site yet be sleek enough to impress international clientele. Smith achieved this delicate balance via details like antique chairs surrounding a Swiss-flag table in the break room and the white-leather Arne Jacobsen Egg that reposes in a lobby corner beneath fiber paintings by area artist Paul Fontana.

If anyone could pull off such a project, SwissTex's husband-wife founders had reasoned, it was Smith: Besides designing the owners' nearby home, she'd been born and raised in the Carpet Capital of the World.

Francis Cauffman

W.L. GORE & ASSOCIATES, ELKTON, MARYLAND

From top: Partitions with bold graphics and soothing natural imagery announce departments, at once dividing and unifying disparate areas. An informal work space, with a plywood accent wall, is configured to accommodate myriad activities. ➤

Business Systems & Technology

Enabling our customers to create competitive advantage through the use of information, systems and technology.

nform

No wonder W.L. Gore keeps landing on *Fortune*'s annual "100 Best Companies to Work For" ranking: It's a model of democracy in action. Staffers who would eventually inhabit the new IT Group office were invited—no, expected to participate in its development and design.

In keeping with the company's nonhierarchical philosophy, Francis Cauffman held workshops in which employees detailed their work needs and ethic. It emerged that they were passionate about their jobs, and most spent long hours at the office. Yet fully one fifth did not require a dedicated space on-site, as they generally conducted business remotely and visited only occasionally.

Armed with this information, the architecture firm created an open floorplan with few fixed walls that—like the company—could adapt agilely to changing demands. The seamless result allows for privacy whether people are working alone or collaborating; at the center of the office is a multifunctional "town center" for socializing, working, and/or eating lunch. Employees requested "honest" and ecofriendly building materials. As many of the staffers are nature lovers, environmental graphics depict images like clouds and blades of grass.

The outcome speaks for itself: For the people, by the people...with thoughtful assistance from Francis Cauffman.

1 WORK AREA

2 INFORMAL GATHERING SPACE

3 TOWN CENTER

4 MEETING ROOM

5 GLOBAL CONNECT

6 LARGE COLLABORATION ROOM

7 ENCLAVE

0   10   20   40

PROJECT TEAM KIM HONG, JOHN CAMPBELL, JULIA LEAHY

PHOTOGRAPHY CHRIS COOPER

www.franciscauffman.com

Clockwise from left:
A muted, almost industrial backdrop alludes to industriousness while bright accents, such as sunny poufs, broadcast creativity at play; polycarbonate panels preserve privacy. A place to grab a quick bite, spread out work, or both. Vivid artwork—an extreme close-up of grass blades—presides over an array of seating vignettes. The monochrome scheme is like an inviting clean white sheet of paper.

20,000 sf

Felderman Keatinge + Associates

ICRETE, BEVERLY HILLS, CALIFORNIA

Clockwise from below: The reception desk transforms as needed—guest check-in, conference table, or layout space for company products. The entry area, with niched troughs for down-lighting, projects both solidity and inventiveness. Workstations remain airily unencumbered, with walnut storage floating before clear glass panels. A typical private office features an FKA-designed desk, fabricated by dTank. A collaborative work space amid individual stations. Another view of the reception area.

Perhaps a book shouldn't be judged by its cover, but it's well understood—even expected—that if innovation is at the heart of your business, your headquarters should reflect it. The client, a company developing new technology for concrete, envisioned a space that could accomplish that— and function as a working office and a product showroom. This think-tank setting would invite interaction and showcase the young firm's cutting-edge green products.

Felderman Keatinge + Associates, charged with executing the project, remained mindful throughout of iCrete's vision and budget. The client leaned aesthetically toward the traditional, and FKA had to strike the right tone, maintaining creative integrity while keeping watch on the bottom line.

Open, fluid, and minimalist, the space is essentially a blank slate, intended to draw co-workers and clients together and stimulate ideas. Visitors are met at the unconventional reception area and ushered to the action at the "hub"; the long reception desk, designed by FKA to multitask, moonlights as a conference table and display site for company products.

In the end, all aims were achieved. The atmosphere is quite sleek indeed, with sculptural and refined architectural elements juxtaposing with the exposed mechanical system. Materials were used imaginatively, combining "quality" and "raw" as iCrete's products do—and in the process creating a space that promotes innovative thinking.

9,189 sf

PROJECT TEAM STANLEY FELDERMAN, NANCY KEATINGE
PHOTOGRAPHY ERIC LAIGNEL (1, 5), STANLEY FELDERMAN/FKA (2–4, 6)
www.fkadesign.com

*Clockwise from
above:* A staircase
just beyond the glass
reception wall links
the two levels; the
company logo offers a
pop of color in an
otherwise stark
space. Italian
manufacturer Fantoni
customized the
mobile benching
system in the main
work area. A Brazilian
rosewood–topped
boardroom table and
console infuse
warmth. A glazed
conference room
maintains the open
aesthetic and sense
of transparency
crucial to the design.
Glass walls separate
the executive office
from the rest of the
design studio, where
a custom shelving
system—displaying
Springs Global
products—divides
core offices.

How does one envision a blank canvas? When the
Brazilian-American home furnishings company Springs
Global sought to relocate its New York operations, it
commissioned MKDA to create a studio/showroom that
would facilitate staff collaboration and showcase products
against a neutral backdrop. However, as the firm was
designing, the client was expanding—exponentially. "They
were growing as we were building," says MKDA president
Michael Kleinberg. "We didn't know if we needed space for
10, 15, or 60 employees."

As a solution, MKDA devised a super-open, flexible layout
that can accommodate changing needs. Custom mobile
furniture by Fantoni allows the studio to reconfigure for
showroom events. A clean, spare palette of whitewashed
wood floors, exposed ceilings, high-gloss white-lacquer
cabinetry, and glass partitions maintains this blank-slate
aesthetic with offices and workrooms set at the core so
as not to block daylight. Brazilian rosewood shelving

delineates offices and provides storage and display space
for products. The use of rosewood, a subtle nod to the
company's national roots, introduces tactility to the hard-
surface space. To head off acoustical issues, designers
employed fabric panels and "clouds" that blend into the
ceilings and absorb sound.

The upshot? "People are energized by the fresh, airy feel
of the space," Kleinberg reports, "and energized employees
make for greater productivity."

MKDA

SPRINGS GLOBAL, NEW YORK

PROJECT TEAM MICHAEL KLEINBERG, LON SKIDDS, EDIN RUDIC,
EDWARD CARDIMONA, DAVID STONE, JOE LIEBER, JOHN O'BRIAN,
WILLIAM AVERSA, KENNETH KLEIMAN, JEANNE RIVKIN

PHOTOGRAPHY ADRIAN WILSON

www.mkda.com

32,000 sf
Renovation

nonprofit & medical

DETERMINED NURTURING
GENUINE HOPEFUL
WELCOMING

There is no organization quite like the Y. The attributes that define our voice convey our relentless quest to help others, our desire to develop people through encouragement, the honest and open fashion that defines our relationships and our belief that we make a difference in our communities each and every day. And finally, when we express ourselves, we want people to understand that the Y is open to all.

How to make the world a better place? That's the concern of these clients, who share a mission to help others—whether via health care, youth support, improved access to education, or philanthropic efforts. Their community-minded approach is reflected in egalitarian work spaces that encourage teamwork and interaction. Common areas are typically programmed to multitask: corridors double as lounges, cafeterias transform into town halls, meeting rooms can be utilized for heads-down work. Transparency is a philosophical imperative, translating to lots of glass and a sense of openness. *We like their worldview.*

M Moser Associates

TEACH FOR AMERICA REGIONAL OFFICE, HOUSTON

To achieve its mission—ensuring impoverished children get a first-class education—Teach For America intensively recruits, trains, and supports teachers for schools in low-income areas. As such, the organization's Houston workplace is less an office than it is a high-performance community center meant to foster a culture of learning and collaboration.

M Moser's engaging scheme, a prototype for future locations, was influenced by sociologist Rawy Oldenburg's notion of a "third place," a neutral public space where communities meet and interact creatively. A flexible open-plan layout facilitates the process. Small rooms that double as office and meeting space—and can be utilized by any staff member for any purpose—are grouped at the core,

freeing the perimeter for clusters of low-partitioned and bench-style workstations that support teamwork and abet the flow of light and air. The use of laptop computers in lieu of desktop models results in even greater density (and fewer cables).

The teacher corps is a mobile population, dropping by the center to mingle, network, and receive professional development outside school hours. Thus copious meeting areas with state-of-the-art AV equipment. A large town hall/café plus a lounge and resource center hosts intimate chats and office-wide forums alike. Conveniently located along circulation routes are casual breakout spaces designed for spontaneous discussions—or quick breathers from the intense job of nurturing young intellects.

Clockwise from left:
Visitors are greeted
by a branding wall
superimposing the
client's clean-lined
logo over an expanse
of raw OSB. The
Bertoia chairs in the
waiting area face a
wall proclaiming the
organization's core
message of first-class
education for all
children. Slices of
plastic tubing
make fun mail slots
for teachers. ➤

16,300 sf
Renovation

```
0   10  20      40
```

1 ENTRY

2 CONFERENCE ROOM

3 TOWN HALL/CAFÉ

4 PRIVATE ROOM

5 LIBRARY/LOUNGE

6 WORKSTATIONS

PROJECT TEAM DAVID WEINBERG, DICK MARKEL, BILL BOUCHEY,
JESSIE BUKEWICZ, MATT ROSSI, HENRY SEXTON

PHOTOGRAPHY JOE C. AKER

www.mmoser.com

Clockwise from opposite top:
Wrapping the core is a series of small private rooms for heads-down work, making phone calls, or one-on-one meetings. The library/ resource center is mostly used after hours for developing lesson plans; its location near the elevator lobby enables it to function as a waiting area. Red accents add a lively touch. The town hall includes stadium seating and a full-service pantry. Bench desking provides flexibility as well as economy of space.

Gary Lee Partners

With over 3,000 visitors a year, the YMCA of the USA is the central office of the nonprofit, providing support to locations across the country. To perform this role, it needed the ability to accommodate groups of differing sizes, often simultaneously. Gary Lee Partners created a sprightly aerie that encourages community and collaboration, with multi-functional rooms, abundant daylight, and myriad gathering zones—spread over three floors—to support interaction.

An added twist, the build-out coincided with the launch of the organization's new identity program; thus the firm was challenged to devise cost-effective means of incorporating these graphics into the design. It treated brand statements as artwork, displayed as posters throughout, including along the walls of a gallerylike circulation route.

An open layout allows for ample teaming areas, while workstations were conceived to give staff members a choice of components for their personal spaces. Employees and visitors can migrate to a café, a lounge area, or reception for brainstorming and socializing. For greater privacy, consultants retreat to sleek hoteling stations.

The headquarters has become a place to work, entertain, inform, and engage. And it can now support YMCA fundraising and educational activities in a manner not previously possible. As a bonus, the project was planned, designed, and built in a rapid 10 months, within the strict budget parameters set by the client.

80,000 sf
LEED Silver

1 RECEPTION/WAITING AREA

2 SUBDIVISIBLE MULTIPURPOSE ROOM

3 CONFERENCE ROOM

4 WORKSTATIONS

5 PRIVATE OFFICE

6 HOTELING STATIONS

0 10 20   40

PROJECT TEAM GARY LEE, DAVID GROUT, DANA KOCH,
TIM SALISBURY, MAURA O'MAHONEY

PHOTOGRAPHY MICHAEL ROBINSON

www.garyleepartners.com

Clockwise from left:
*Workstations adjacent
to meeting tables
spark collaboration.
The café provides an
intimate setting where
employees can dine
and interact. Training
and conference rooms
are flexible and high-
tech, with operable
walls for subdividing.
The open-layout
work spaces are
emboldened by
bright panels.*

Ted Moudis Associates

46,000 sf
Renovation

Clockwise from top:
A Japanese lantern–style light fixture crowns seventh-floor reception. One flight up, an explosive chandelier faces off against a rigorous seating vignette; glass walls and a shoji-like privacy screen define the space. Structural columns support a wood-veneer counter in the lunchroom. Mozambique wood was chosen for office fronts because of its intriguing variegated grain. A view of the eighth and ninth floors. Reception on the eighth floor.

NONPROFIT ORGANIZATION, NEW YORK

Take three organizations, give each a floor in a Fifth Avenue landmark building, and create a trio of environments that share a language yet exhibit distinct personalities: With this formidable project, Ted Moudis Associates took on the challenge. Accent colors first appear to be scarce, but who minds when everything is this bright, airy, and expansive?

Look closer, though, and subtle differences emerge. The seventh floor—home to a philanthropic group devoted to mathematics, theoretical computer science and physics, and autism research—showcases organic forms, embodied by reception's curved desk and soft amber pendant. The informal work environment unfolds in layers of hushed natural color and copious light wood.

The domain of the eighth-floor organization is math as well, but its aim is to elevate the teaching of the subject in U.S. public schools by recruiting, training, and retaining practitioners. Details nod to the group's focus: A geometric pendant hangs in reception, and distraction strips on glass walls bear mathematical formulas. Slightly deeper finishes prevail as soft brown tones contrast with white casegoods.

On the ninth floor, an investment firm provides services for its entrepreneurial endeavors. Fittingly, the design is more polished and refined, with the richest, boldest colors of all employed alongside dark walnut furnishings.

The common thread between the offices, literally linking them, is an exquisite floating staircase. Then there's the abundance of wood and light and the effortless-seeming sleek simplicity. Surely nonprofit has never looked so good.

PROJECT TEAM TED MOUDIS, CHRISTOPHER SAVOGLOU, MITCHELL ROSS, JACQUELINE BARR, MICHAEL SINKEW, DANIELLE SINGER, KIMBERLY SHARPE
PHOTOGRAPHY ERIC LAIGNEL
www.tedmoudis.com

Cuningham Group Architecture

EPIC SYSTEMS CORPORATION HEADQUARTERS
VERONA, WISCONSIN

The campus of this medical-software management company boasts rolling green pastures, grazing horses, and a bright red barn. But lest you mistake the vibe as provincial, note the sign welcoming guests to "Epic Intergalactic Headquarters."

The client set out to prove that global reach and a small carbon footprint could go hand in hand. Sustainability was the driver behind Cuningham Group's scheme for the 812-acre site, which includes a learning center and the mixed-use Campus Two. Among the eco-conscious elements: underground parking to minimize the impact on natural vegetation, some 3,576 geothermal wells, seven acres of photovoltaic cells, on-site retention ponds, bio-swales, occupancy and daylight sensors, verdant roofs, and regionally manufactured and sourced materials.

The architectural style acknowledges the local vernacular. Amply glazed façades pair local Kasota limestone with barn-red metal panels and zinc-coated copper cladding. Inside, spaces feel rich yet have a Zen-like calm, with plentiful daylight and views of surrounding farmland.

Collaboration and focused individual tasks are prioritized in equal measure: Every one of Epic's 5,100 employees gets a private office, while group work is supported by cozy teaming spaces with woodburning fireplaces. Other spots for congregating include a treehouse (actually a conference room, made primarily of recycled construction waste), various themed meeting areas, and even a slide. At every point, the design reinforces Epic's humorously plainspoken credo: Do good, have fun, and make money. They might consider adding "and enjoy the architecture."

Clockwise from top: The learning center's lush courtyard fosters impromptu chats. Bases are built from Kasota, a limestone native to the Midwest. The reception area of the learning center, which houses classrooms, conference and seminar areas, break-out spaces, vendor displays, pre-function pavilions, and an auditorium that seats 5,400. Colored zinc panels face the exterior of Campus Two. A gathering space in the same building. A "pop-up" entry to the below-ground parking.

983,287 sf (learning center)
670,000 sf (Campus Two)
760,000 sf (3,458-car parking structure)

PROJECT TEAM JOHN CUNINGHAM, NINA BROADHURST, CHAD CLOW, MICHAEL BERG, LANI PRIDDY, THERESA ANDREWS, MATTHEW MURRAY
PHOTOGRAPHY GEORGE HEINRICH (1–3), DANA WHEELOCK (4–6)
www.cuningham.com

Rapt Studio

ACTELION PHARMACEUTICALS
SOUTH SAN FRANCISCO

Actelion presented Rapt with an ambitious project brief for its U.S. outpost. First, the Basel-based biopharmaceutical company wanted the space to reflect its Swiss DNA while nodding to local Bay Area culture. Second, the client's wish to prioritize employee retention led to varied amenities such as copious gathering spaces, a fitness center, and a full-service café. Third, Actelion leadership hoped to nurture relationships between departments that would be spread over multiple floors and realign divisions that had become separated through company growth.

Answering many of those desires is Rapt's free-flowing layout, inspired by the concept of membrane porosity, a term borrowed from cell biology. Cityscape analogies also inform the scheme. A large lobby was conceived as a piazza that would unify the building's north and south wings. A central pathway, known as the boulevard, connects a series of plazas that surround stairways; other informal breakout spots along this circulation route encourage casual catch-ups. Many common spaces perform double duty: Conference rooms act as buffer zones between main corridors and work areas, while the café accommodates both dining and meeting functions.

In addition to offering abundant and flexible space for collaboration, the headquarters supports solitary pursuits like brainstorming. When staffers need to turn their attention inward, they can contemplate the San Francisco Bay through expansive window walls or, better yet, while strolling along waterfront nature trails.

Clockwise from above: Pete Sans's Ameba pendants add verve to reception, floored in polished concrete. A glass-sided staircase rises over an informal breakout spot. An Interlam wall panel adds texture along the boulevard.

42,000 sf
New construction
LEED Silver

PROJECT TEAM RAPT STUDIO: DAVID GALULLO, RICHARD POLLACK, CHRISTINE SHAW, HAKEE CHANG, KRISTIN TIERNAN, COLLEEN KIRKLAND, LYDIA CHAN. ACTELION PHARMACEUTICALS: GEOFF GRANT
GENERAL CONTRACTOR DPR CONSTRUCTION
MEP ENGINEER AMIT WADHWA & ASSOCIATES
STRUCTURAL ENGINEER KPFF
KITCHEN CONSULTANT CINI LITTLE
AUDIOVISUAL CONSULTANT SNADER & ASSOCIATES
PHOTOGRAPHY ERIC LAIGNEL

www.raptstudio.com

Clockwise from opposite top: A waterfront collaborative space is furnished with Steelcase's Media: scape system and Patricia Urquiola's Last Minute stools; walls coated in IdeaPaint render them writeable. Red cedar clads the entry to the staff café, Bistro by the Bay. The gym. In the boulevard, cork-rubber flooring and energy-efficient Neo lamps with swivel connectors provide the backdrop for vignettes of Andreu World chairs and Vue tables, by Jang Won Yoon for Bernhardt. A reconfigurable meeting room has conference tables by Datesweiser. A staircase along the boulevard.

Cannon Design

UNIVERSITY HEALTHSYSTEM CONSORTIUM, CHICAGO

Clockwise from right:
Huge irises lining a wall in the boardroom, the "cortex" of the consortium, suggest a brightness of vision. In reception, rolling screens emerge from a wall pocket to create a boardroom waiting area. Another moveable screen, in the well-situated café, was designed with bronchi in mind. Glass walls dividing private offices abet the flow of light. The mosaic feature wall in the café. Chandeliers modeled on firing synapses illuminate an elevator lobby.

77,000 sf
LEED Silver

Who would've thought a building could have a nervous system? Well, the University HealthSystem Consortium's does, and it makes sense. When UHC decided to relocate its headquarters, the interiors had to reflect the group's mission, which is allying major U.S. academic medical centers, affiliated hospitals, and healthcare professionals. Cannon Design took on the project and came up with a novel concept: The guiding design narrative would be human physiology—a theme that was only natural for a group with connections at its heart.

Bodily systems play out architecturally according to each space's function. Bone-marrow cells served as aesthetic inspiration for elements in the break area on the main level. In the second-floor break area, motifs draw from respiratory cells. The screened entry, curving glass-mosaic wall, and geometric ceiling fixtures in the large café—the inevitable nucleus of staff activity—all reference bronchi.

On the third floor, the nervous system is interpreted via lighting techniques and spatial interconnectivity. Chandeliers suggest firing synapses, and privacy screens that roll on a ceiling track recall neurons. On the wall of the boardroom, the facility's cortex, a row of startling stylized irises hints at a broad vision. Talk about eye-opening design!

PROJECT TEAM BARBARA RIESKE, MARK C. HIRONS, CATHY RITZ, NOELLE C. KINYON, DAVID A. CARR, ERIC WYSZKOWSKI
PHOTOGRAPHY CHRISTOPHER BARRETT
www.cannondesign.com

law

Think law firms are inherently law-abiding? Think again. Case studies in rule breaking, these projects cast aside many typical office trappings. Spatial hierarchy is subverted. Practice groups are intermingled not Balkanized. Millwork-and-stone palettes look fresh, not fusty. Infrastructure is anticipatory. And floorplans are blown wide open—even as they uphold the crucial need for client and employee privacy. *The verdict: Barely legal.*

Cuningham
Group
Architecture

NILAN JOHNSON LEWIS, MINNEAPOLIS

Glass-wrapped Midcentury skyscrapers are a bit like water towers and hot-dog carts: Ubiquitous in New York City, they're altogether rare in a place like Minneapolis. So when the architects at Cuningham Group first saw the future site of the Nilan Johnson Lewis law offices—which they'd been hired to gut renovate—their attention quickly shifted to the 11½-foot floor-to-ceiling windows. Grouping common spaces along the perimeter ensured democratic access to vistas, including a bird's-eye view of a plaza used for summertime tennis-tournament matches (love that).

Further preserving sight lines are slim 1950s furnishings that reiterate the modernist vibe. In another nod to the existing architecture, private offices feature glass walls with attenuated wood frames. But the architects selected materials with an eye less on the building itself and more on the ethos of its newest occupants. "It's a progressive law firm, highly dedicated to its clients," explains project manager Sara Weiner. "The fundamental characteristic of integrity became the analogy for our design approach." That translated to avoiding plastic and relying heavily on solid wood, quartz, and concrete. Which made snagging LEED-CI certification a lot easier—not to mention a favorable verdict from the firm's most important jury: its clients.

77,000 sf
LEED-CI

PROJECT TEAM JOHN CUNINGHAM, SARA WEINER, CHAD CLOW, TOM KYLLO, THERESA ANDREWS, SHAWN OLSON, TED STEINER
PHOTOGRAPHY DANA WHEELOCK
www.cuningham.com

Clockwise from opposite: Entry is gained via a warm, walnut-lined reception whose dichroic-glass wall has a steel-mesh overlay to give the effect of a water feature. The layout revolves around clusters of open and closed office spaces that serve various practice groups. The heart of the space, the "connection," is a lunchroom with lounge and dining areas intended to embody the firm's laid-back culture. The boardroom—part of a two-floor conference area—gets a visual boost from a back-painted glass tabletop. In lieu of an art collection, the architects used graphic lighting features and sleek furniture to liven common spaces.

Like many a Hollywood success story, Century City had humble beginnings: The L.A. neighborhood was once a 20th Century Fox backlot. Fast-forward and it's a bustling business center, home to Fox headquarters, ICM, the Creative Artists Agency, and numerous media-related legal establishments, Morris Yorn now included. The move from a small loft in Santa Monica to a high-rise in the district marked a milestone in the entertainment law firm's own success story.

The objective was to create an office with the look and feel of a high-powered talent agency, giving its film-business clientele a home away from home for relaxed meetings and discussions. Comfortable it is, but by no

Felderman Keatinge + Associates

MORRIS YORN, CENTURY CITY, CALIFORNIA

means casual. Artwork, lighting, and a preponderance of pebbles hint at organic-chic leanings, but the space is sleek and understated, with a dignified earth-tone palette and white accents. Natural wood grains, stainless steel, and glass panels are hallmarks of the design.

Contemporary and earthy, the carefully curated furnishings also exude some Golden Age glamour. Vertical blinds are used throughout. Extensive files are tucked away in handsome millwork storage units. A feng shui specialist was consulted, to excellent effect: Calming white space abounds. The impression is subdued and grounded, spare and complete, uplifting and serene, with sweeping views as good as any in a silver-screen office scene.

Clockwise from opposite top: The raised reception area as seen from the elevator lobby; the Ingo Maurer chandeliers incorporate Stanley Felderman's drawings. Motorized drapery lining the Egg conference room affords flexible privacy. In the main conference room, a river-rock inset on the trapezoidal table houses technology controls. The lounge/ client meeting area, with multimedia wall and concealed coffee bar, is easily curtained off. FKA-designed workstations were fabricated locally— by dTank—in walnut and fumed oak with glass and metal privacy panels. The reception seating "stage" features a leather carpet inset, bundled-wood coffee tables, a pebble border, and bronze planters with mini rock gardens.

24,906 sf
Completed in 14 weeks
Screening room, bar, café, game room

PROJECT TEAM STANLEY FELDERMAN, NANCY KEATINGE
PHOTOGRAPHY ERIC LAIGNEL (1, 2, 4, 6), BENNY CHAN/FOTOWORKS (3, 5)
www.fkadesign.com

Goettsch Partners

JENNER & BLOCK, CHICAGO

Relocating to the top 14 floors of a build-to-suit high-rise afforded this elite law firm the opportunity to design a new office, one that showed its clients an even more confident, authoritative face. Goettsch Partners accomplished that objective with a smart, classic scheme that makes use of iconic furnishings and luxe materials.

Metaphors abound. Reception seating was conceived as a "passionate dialogue" between Eileen Gray and Le Corbusier, meant to symbolize Jenner & Block's commitment to discourse and diversity. Sleek, expansive swaths of travertine, backlit onyx, and high-polished marble were chosen to "reflect the client's clarity of legal thought and practice," the architects explain.

Stainless-steel frames embrace the frosted-glass walls of conference rooms, which are punctuated with overscale leather-clad pivot doors. Glass and aluminum distinguishes the façades of attorneys' offices, establishing a continuity of finishes. Surrounding the core, a unified stretch of flex space housing paralegals, case rooms, and secretarial clusters is defined by demountable glazed partitions— they can be repositioned to adapt to changing caseload requirements. (The furniture is modular, too.) Wood ceiling canopies soften the more austere surfaces, and historic Le Corbusier paint colors liven the cafés.

Energy-efficient lighting is one of many strategies the architects employed to fulfill the firm's earth-friendly aims. Case closed: The project earned LEED Gold.

Clockwise from above: Demountable glass walls and modular furniture create a reconfigurable flex zone. Double walls of frosted glass allow privacy while admitting daylight; conference rooms are accessed via oversize pivot doors surfaced in leather. The millwork and stone floors in reception provide a quietly dramatic setting for modern classics. A food-service café is housed in a cross-floor pass-through. Backlit onyx panels announce a pair of multiuse rooms. ➤

From top: Travertine fronts the reception desk and clads nearby feature walls; glowing onyx and rich leather inject warmth. In meeting rooms, technology is integrated into custom conference tables, allowing all present optimal viewing angles.

PROJECT TEAM JIM PRENDERGAST, RUSSELL MANTHY, CHERI JACOBS, AUSTIN ZIKE, ANDREW TARCIN, RANDALL CHAPPLE, ADY CHU, JC SANCHEZ, MICHAEL BYUN, KATE PUVOGEL, MARLENA BANKS, JUSTINE BIRMINGHAM, PAO LERTSIRI

PHOTOGRAPHY CHRISTOPHER BARRETT (1, 4), STEVE HALL/HEDRICH BLESSING (2, 3, 5–7)

www.gpchicago.com

1 PARTNERS' OFFICES

2 ASSOCIATES' OFFICES

3 CASE ROOMS

4 CONFERENCE ROOMS

5 SUPPORT FUNCTIONS

6 PARALEGAL STATIONS

7 SECRETARIAL STATIONS

0   20   40   80

TPG Architecture

SHEPPARD, MULLIN, RICHTER & HAMPTON, NEW YORK

Clockwise from right: Glass-front conference rooms allow views of adjacent spaces, reception included. The airy entry features a circular custom reception desk, terrazzo flooring, and a staircase illuminated by an Ingo Maurer fixture. Squared-off reception chairs contrast with the organically patterned Tai Ping rug. Vignettes splashed with contemporary color—such as this trio of orange Bernhardt chairs—are sprinkled throughout the main level. The glass-rail stair connects the 38th and 39th floors.

Evidence that 30 Rock isn't exactly as it looks on the small screen: this law firm's elegantly sober office, which occupies one and a half floors of the iconic (both architecturally and pop culturally) Midtown address. TPG Architecture was charged with creating an open, light-filled, and comfortable aerie—and that it did.

The design team maximized ceiling heights by attending to the use of ambient lighting, carefully coordinating mechanical systems, and putting side-feed air conditioning in perimeter offices. Because one of the client's founding principles is to provide high-quality but cost-effective legal services, custom details are top-notch without shouting top-dollar. The reception desk is enlivened by rich wood fins; a dramatic Ingo Maurer chandelier accents a nearby feature stair; tailored furnishings and crisp window treatments contribute understated excellence; jolts of color from rugs and furnishings pop against a predominantly pale palette. Ample use of glass, meanwhile, supports the firm's policy of transparency.

TPG also de-emphasized the reception-area TV; you'll have to catch Tina Fey elsewhere.

PROJECT TEAM JIM PHILLIPS, ALEX LEMBERGER, FLORENCIA KRATSMAN, ALLISON HOPKE
PHOTOGRAPHY CHRIS COOPER
www.tpgarchitecture.com

Clockwise from above: A vignette of leather armchairs supports impromptu gatherings; the fiery hue in the abstract area rug is a company hallmark. In reception, glass-top tables flank wire-frame chairs. Louvered slats screen a formal conference room. The staff lunchroom, near the window wall, is adjacent to the lunch center so plumbing, catering, and refrigeration can be shared.

Nelson

SEYFARTH SHAW, ATLANTA

The explosive growth of Seyfarth Shaw's local office, along with a desire for a space better reflecting its brand image, led the law firm to Nelson...and this new Midtown office. Flexibility and efficiency were top priorities, so Nelson devised a scheme both bright and modern, with consistent design elements and technologies easily adapted and reinterpreted should the firm expand further.

Unexpected fixture variations and tactile materials are a common theme. European glass pendants augment sleek, minimalist task lighting. High-contrast materials lend dimension and depth, and invigorating touches of Seyfarth Shaw's signature red recur, adding allure.

Much of the innovation can be credited to a layout with well thought-out adjacencies. Instead of being situated by practice areas, attorneys' offices are dispersed throughout the space, to enable cross selling and promote client relationship-building. Each private office measures 160 square feet, a modest dimension that results in 48 attorneys per floor. Workstations for legal secretaries were designed to ensure acoustic and visual privacy while encouraging communication and collaboration. The stations are close to areas supporting such tasks as printing and filing, an arrangement that facilitates cross training, equipment sharing, balancing of workload, and heightened productivity.

Amenities multitask as well: Upscale finishes and audiovisual equipment mean the sleek lunchroom can function as a meeting space beyond peak mealtime.

68,000 sf
LEED Gold

PROJECT TEAM MARTY FESTENSTEIN, CHRIS LIU,
AMBER FRAZIER, TIM MOLE, MORRIE SPANG, CHRIS
HATFIELD, JOON KIM, MIKE CHURCHILL, MATT RODIE

PHOTOGRAPHY HALKIN PHOTOGRAPHY

www.nelsononline.com

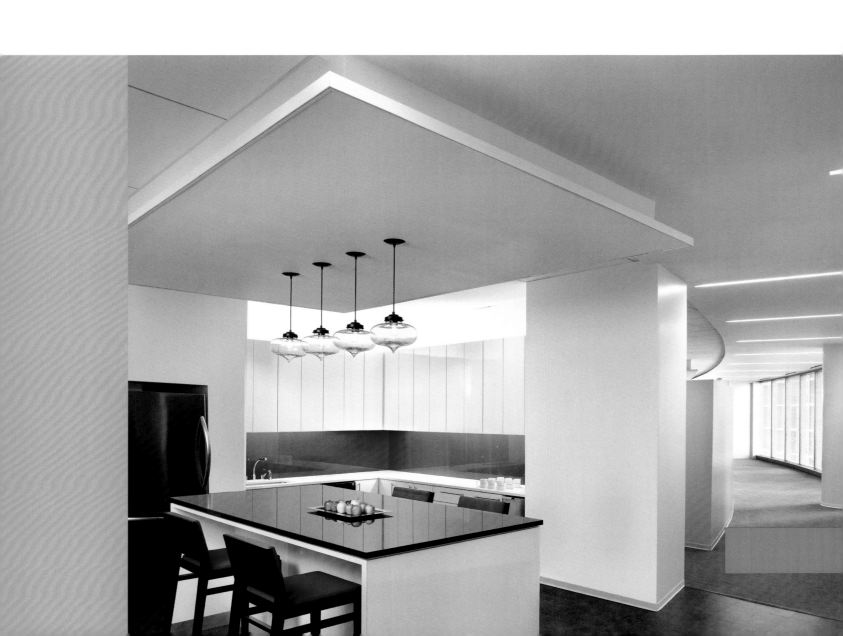

TWG LAW LOFT, NEW YORK

Studio Tractor

When an established Manhattan law firm hires an upstart Brooklyn-based architecture studio to build its offices, you know the client is after more than just a new decor. Indeed, the partners of Thompson, Wigdor & Gilly selected Studio Tractor because they wanted a design blueprint that would do no less than reinvent the firm identity.

The airy, dynamic space, in the Flatiron district, possessed an industrial rawness that Studio Tractor copartners Michael Tower and Mark Kolodziejczak sought to preserve. Exquisitely detailed natural finishes lend sophistication without eradicating the sense of patina. The two maneuvered around cast-iron columns, wood window frames, and exposed steam radiators, applying coats of smooth plaster to walls and ceilings and installing white-oak flooring. The full-height glass partitions fronting perimeter offices allow sunlight to filter deep into the floor plate, heightening the impact of fresh-faced surfaces.

A few well-placed touches lend liveliness—and indicate to clients that they've arrived at a different sort of law firm. The luminescent blue glass fronting the white Corian reception desk echoes the company's logo. A feature wall and elevator portal cut from slabs of honed New York bluestone add gravitas. Furnishings such as a Goetz sofa for one partner and an Arts and Crafts desk for another speak to the singular tastes and attentions of the firm.

Clockwise from above: A floating partition, made of Douglas fir panels with an exposed steel frame, feels solid but weightless—and separates reception from a run of offices. A series of vertical slot lights animate the austere north corridor. Box sofas by Autobahn furnish reception; the custom blue-tinted panels are by Port Richmond Glass. A table and chairs by Charles and Ray Eames ground the glass-enclosed lunchroom, designed to appear as a glowing volume.

8,000 sf
Renovation

1 RECEPTION

2 MEETING ROOMS

3 SHARED OFFICE

4 PARTNER'S OFFICE

5 LUNCHROOM

6 WORKSTATIONS

0   10   20   40

PROJECT TEAM MARK KOLODZIEJCZAK, MICHAEL TOWER, ANDREW BARWICK

PHOTOGRAPHY CHUCK CHOI

www.studiotractor.com

Clockwise from left:
The conference zone can be divided in two via a retractable walnut wall. A wood-clad ceiling warms the bright, window-wrapped space. A partner's office features a Miro desk, a pair of Eero Saarinen Executive chairs, and Castore suspension lamps; flooring throughout is white oak. Walnut details are repeated in the southern corridor, where vertical end caps punctuate the glass walls.

WilliamsCraig

CRAWLEY MEREDITH BRUSH, TORONTO

Clockwise from above: In a meeting room, an arched wrought-iron window surrounded by exposed brick offers an element of drama. Castor Design's Recycled fluorescent-tube light floats above the custom gray-oak library table; artwork and classic Aluminum Group chairs add a punch of color. For privacy, a series of sliding panels—in natural-finish rift-cut white oak—close off the library and café from reception; at rear, a communal island supports casual interaction. ➤

It isn't unusual to seek inspiration at an art institution. But when contemplating the design of its new law office, CMB found an unexpected muse in a nearby institution itself: the Art Gallery of Ontario, a daring swoop of titanium and glass masterminded by Frank Gehry. CMB's top-floor space had an unobstructed view of the avant-garde façade, which is reminiscent of a ship's exposed hull. To preserve sight lines, WilliamsCraig devised an industrial-luxe scheme with much glazing, adding transparency both literally and figuratively.

Slicing through the center of the floor plate, a long run of public spaces—encompassing reception, library, and café—is separated from the elevator lobby by a glass wall. A skylight floods these areas with sunshine, as does the full-height arched window that forms a striking backdrop to a client meeting area. Perimeter offices are enclosed in glass so that even legal assistants toiling in interior workstations can enjoy the sight of Gehry's showstopper.

A palette of wide-plank gray-oak floors and rift-cut white-oak millwork complements the rawer existing textures, such as brick walls and rustic beams stripped of glossy finishes. The latter two original features capture the design philosophy in a nutshell: honest, strong, and true.

8,300 sf
Renovation

1 RECEPTION

2 LIBRARY

3 CAFÉ

4 PARTNER'S OFFICE

5 MEETING ROOM

6 BOARDROOM

7 WORKING ROOM

0   10   20   40

PROJECT TEAM KAREN WILLIAMS, JOELLE CRAIG, STEPHANIE WONG, JENN DUGUAY, JAMIE GRUENWALD, OLGA MELNIKOVA

PHOTOGRAPHY TOM ARBAN

www.williamscraigdesign.com

Clockwise from left:
The low workstation partitions preserve openness; the storage volume separating the café and library from the work area features shelving on both sides. A series of Tom Dixon pressed-glass pendants shed light on the café island. A glass wall separates the elevator lobby from a continuous public zone including reception, the library, and the café. A dropped drywall ceiling over the main boardroom table minimizes sound transmission; an area rug composed of carpet tiles anchors the scene.

office mix

What do these spaces have in common?   Like their designs, these companies defy

categorization. But bright and airy rules the day:

Natural light is maximized and shared by all. Partitions are low, ceilings high; glass is in, Sheetrock out. Atria, art, and jolts of

color keep the eye entertained. Floating staircases connect floors and people, too, sparking collaboration. Spots for working

solo or as part of a team abound; cafés are the new greet, eat, and meet zone, and mod pods are a hotbed of creativity.

With the next big idea right around the corner, why would you ever leave?

Elliott + Associates
Architects

CHESAPEAKE ENERGY CORPORATION
OKLAHOMA CITY

Clockwise from below: The firm's latest project at the Chesapeake campus features an office building that unfolds around a central atrium. The glass-front Building 13 and steel-paneled garage are visually unified by matching sun screens. Panels of iridescent dichroic acrylic form the atrium's 115-foot-long sculpture. ➤

Architect Rand Elliott and Chesapeake CEO Aubrey McClendon have quite a history together. Over the last 23 years, the two have collaborated on myriad projects, a number of them here on the energy company's sprawling campus. When Chesapeake's explosive growth called for the acquisition of 24 adjacent acres, Elliott was summoned once again—this time to envision an office building with attached car park at the highest-visibility corner of the new site.

The design celebrates the power of color and light to lend the structures a kinetic energy. Building 13 is a skinny triangle with the longest wall in glass, terminating on both corners at a stair tower. Motorists and pedestrians can see in, while staffers, ascending or descending, see out.

The interior revolves around a triangular skylit atrium, a feature that derives from Chesapeake's egalitarian culture. Everyone, support staff included, gets a similarly sized private office; the entire campus shares the same 52-foot module. Furthermore, each work space was designed with a window. Offices inboard of the double-loaded corridors offer views of the atrium's showpiece: a stunning swirl of hues dancing in sunbeams. Elliott achieved this rainbow effect via a ceiling-hung installation of dichroic acrylic panels, joined with hinges to form an immense squiggle. Colors are in constant flux, shifting with the seasons, the time of day, and the viewer's vantage point.

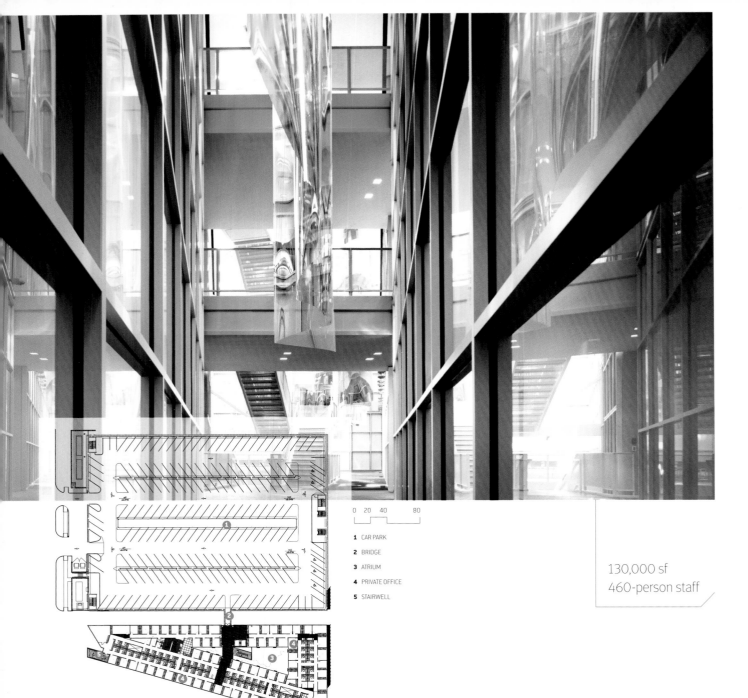

0 20 40 80

1 CAR PARK

2 BRIDGE

3 ATRIUM

4 PRIVATE OFFICE

5 STAIRWELL

130,000 sf
460-person staff

PROJECT TEAM BUILDING 13: RAND ELLIOTT, MICHAEL HOFFNER, SAM MOORE.
CAR PARK: RAND ELLIOTT, BILL YEN, MIHO KOLLIOPOULOS, MICHAEL HOFFNER

PHOTOGRAPHY SCOTT MCDONALD/HEDRICH BLESSING

www.e-a-a.com

***Clockwise from
opposite:*** *Walking up
or down the switch-
back staircase alters
one's perception of
the sculpture; tables
and stacking chairs
can be used to
transform the atrium
into a conference
center. Private offices
surround the atrium.
The car park is clad
in panels of painted,
insulated steel. The
bridge between the
car park and office
is constructed of
perforated steel. The
anodized-aluminum
frames of the atrium's
glass walls enhance
reflectivity.*

Call it a tale of two businesses: A Kuwait-based real-estate developer initiated an ambitious headquarters project under the leadership of Yvonne Colacion, then a vice president at RTKL International. When the designer's corporate interiors division at RTKL Los Angeles fell prey to the economic downturn, the client was loathe to let her get away. In fact, the Tamdeen Group thought so highly of Colacion, the firm urged her to open her own studio and continue shepherding the project.

Fortunately for everyone involved, she did. Light is a focus—visitors often find themselves surrounded by or walking toward it—and Colacion proved a master manipulator, factoring in how silhouettes and shadows would fall. The neutral palette works well as backdrop for the "on-display" concept the team developed: a stage of sorts on which to showcase modern design while upholding a progressive Arab cultural heritage. Interiors are muted but never bland, somber not stuffy, elegant without pretension; many details allude to intricate elements of Moorish architecture.

In a reflection of Tamdeen's embrace of diversity, flexibility, and the future, Colacion designed open-plan areas and raised-floor and -ceiling systems to accommodate constant change—of staff, job responsibilities, technology, even company organizational structure.

The tale of these two companies ends happily, with both parties rating the project a resounding success.

Colacion Studio

TAMDEEN GROUP, KUWAIT CITY

Clockwise from opposite: Korban Flaubert's aluminum Cell Screen divides the two-story reception area, filtering sunlight and casting intriguing shadows; its pattern echoes that of the Moorish-inflected rug. A teak staircase fairly floats between floors 4 and 5. Detail of the suspended Cell Screen. The vertical garden treatment in the ground-floor VIP reception repeats in the upstairs reception, creating the illusion that the feature extends through the building. ➤

PROJECT TEAM YVONNE COLACION, MANDY CHAN, DWOYNE KEITH, NORA LEE, JASON LITT

ARCHITECT OF RECORD SSH INTERNATIONAL

PHOTOGRAPHY ERIC LAIGNEL

www.colacionstudio.com

55,000 sf
New construction

Clockwise from left:
The self-contained open office area, with Haworth seating and workstations and adorned ductwork, imparts an almost Space Age vibe. A fifth-floor "veranda" meeting room, enclosed by a sculptural partition, has outdoor access. A counter and cabinets stretch across one wall of the fifth-floor lunchroom, which is open to the veranda meeting/ conference center. Etched on the frosted glass marking an executive office is a motif that recurs in various forms. The entry to the veranda meeting rooms is clad in LED-lit teak strips.

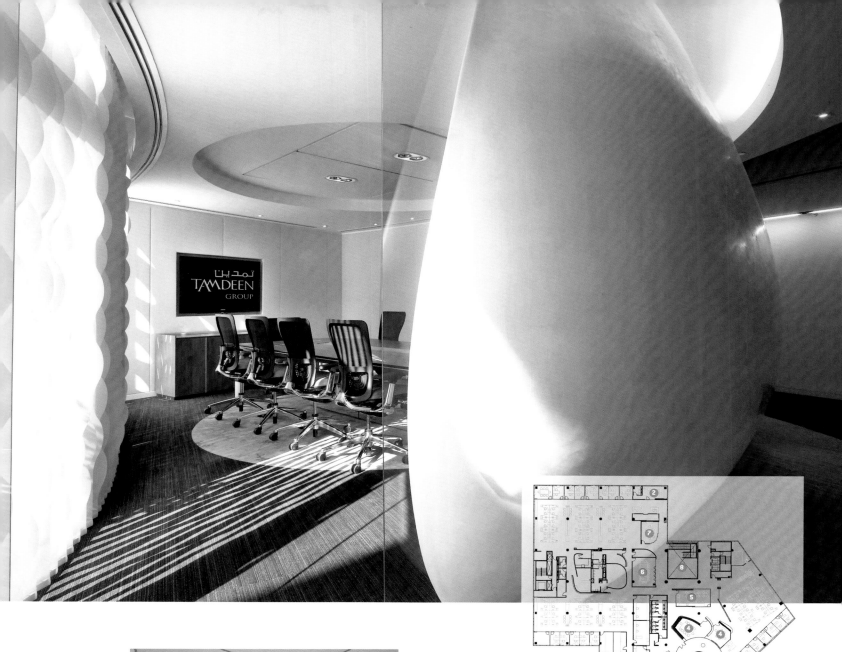

1 5TH-FLOOR RECEPTION

2 EXECUTIVE OFFICE

3 OUTDOOR AREA

4 VERANDA MEETING ROOM

5 LUNCHROOM

6 MULTIPURPOSE ROOM

7 CONFERENCE ROOM

8 OVERLOOK TO 4TH-FLOOR RECEPTION

WCIT Architecture

KIEWIT BUILDING GROUP, HONOLULU

Headquartered in a former Dole pineapple cannery, this Hawaiian construction company wanted to initiate a renovation that would celebrate the history of the building—and also motivate the designers and engineers who'd work in it. WCIT Architecture was enlisted to do the honors.

The design team reworked the compartmentalized floorplan so the dreary two-story structure would feel airy and bright. The ground-floor lobby and reception was expanded to incorporate a flex space, which can remain open for parties or be enclosed by sliding glass panels for meetings. Nearby, workstations and breakout areas are defined by low partitions that offer a hint of privacy as they encourage a spirit of collaboration among staffers.

That ambience carries through to the second level, where glazed walls front a conference room and private offices. An atrium keeps the heart of the loftlike building clear and the employees visually connected. In a whimsical nod to the cannery days, a translucent feature wall—in juicy yellow, the company's logo color—makes the atrium glow. It rises up behind the metal staircase and folds over to form a ceiling canopy, where it supports a sculptural chandelier. An elegant twist of industrial cables, the fixture pays homage to the building's new role as a conduit for interconnectedness.

From top: Offices and meeting rooms cluster around a central atrium, which keeps the two-story space feeling lofty. The knotted chandelier, a custom commission, is a metaphor of sorts for the renovation concept: Functional and flexible, it signifies the power in—and importance of—joining forces. ⬎

1 RECEPTION

2 CONFERENCE ROOM/FLEX SPACE

3 WORKSTATIONS

4 COMMON WORK AREA

5 KITCHEN

5,500 sf
$815,000 budget

0   10   20   40

Clockwise from left:
The feature wall, made with panels of 3Form resin, injects bright color into an otherwise neutral work space. Gracious and modern, the reception area features polished dyed-concrete floors and a custom desk fronted in solid surface. Low-wattage bulbs keep the chandelier glowing. On the second floor, glazed office partitions by Steelcase encourage employee interaction.

PROJECT TEAM ROB IOPA, LISA MARIA PRIESTER, REUBEN CHOCK, PAUL NIIYAMA, ROCKY MARQUEZ
PHOTOGRAPHY DAVID MOORE

www.wcitarch.com

Box Studios

NEWMONT MINING CORPORATION, DENVER

The client, an established international corporation, needed to consolidate four locations in a single new headquarters that would transform the office culture, meet high expectations for quality, and embrace sustainabilty—all on a tight timeline and within the landlord's tenant-improvement allowance. Box Studios answered those needs and then some, creating an elegant, light-filled workplace that's both highly functional and appealing to all generations.

The office occupies seven floors of a new LEED-Gold building. Although schedule constraints precluded additional certification for the interior remodel, there are green features aplenty: energy-efficient lighting, a flexible universal layout, views for all employees, Cradle to Cradle—certified carpet tile, nontoxic millwork from certified forests, employee showers, and Greenguard-certified furniture with 40 percent recycled content.

A prevailing sense of openness symbolizes the client's commitment to teamwork and transparency while helping redefine a company vision that is inclusive for all. Blocks of same-size workstations with low partitions act as egalitarian dividers, preserving expansive views and natural light. In a departure from old-school corporate hierarchy, perimeter corners are mostly given over to bright collaborative spaces rather than enclosed private quarters. Clear glass office fronts are detailed with bronze rods that lend a jewelrylike touch. Thoughtful details like uplifted ceilings and vibrant finishes are repeated throughout.

Modern, cohesive, and inspiring: We award the new decor a gold star.

PROJECT TEAM LYNN COIT, LAUREN DUNDON, JIM GRACZYK, DAVID FOSTER, KAYE MULLANEY
PHOTOGRAPHY BRAD GILLETTE
www.bxstudios.com

Clockwise from opposite: Glass mosaics in saturated hues arc over the lunchroom, while slotted openings mimic skylights. Knoll workstations with low dividers preserve panoramic vistas and access to natural light. Veneer soffits and drum pendants repeat visual themes found elsewhere. Extensive daylight, expansive views, transparent planes, and gleaming surfaces reflect the client's credo of openness and transparency. A casual meeting area is convenient to an administrative center detailed with figured veneer and a block of white Corian. The 24-seat boardroom employs integrated technology, vaulted ceilings, and suspended lighting to frame the mountain backdrop.

215,000 sf
New construction

M Moser Associates

NOKIA SIEMENS NETWORKS
NOIDA, INDIA

Mobile broadband company NSN is at the forefront of the communications business. So it's no surprise that buzzwords like connection, engagement, and exchange informed the design of its Global Services Business headquarters. A fluid and flexible floorplan oriented around double-height volumes and multitasking spaces supports the company's collaborative ethos while meeting the divergent needs of in-house and mobile staffers alike.

One of M Moser's most effective gestures was to unite the two levels with an internal staircase that encourages spontaneous encounters and idea sharing. For a similar reason, conference and meeting rooms were sited to be convenient to all corners of the space. For conversations between participants scattered across the globe, a high-definition videoconferencing room—dubbed the halo—supports real-time, face-to-face interactions.

Angled within the grid of teamwork-friendly benching desks are breakout hubs geared to intimate brainstorming sessions; these collaboration zones also corral office equipment like photocopiers and printers. Catering to roving staffers who spend a majority of time off-site are amenities such as hoteling stations, private lockers, baggage rooms, and travel help desks.

The client's commitment to sustainability and to creating a healthy work environment inspired ecofriendly and energy-efficient touches like low-VOC paints and finishes, low-consumption fixtures, recyclable materials, and segregation of nonrenewable waste. At NSN headquarters, high speed goes hand in hand with high-minded.

165,000 sf
LEED Gold

Clockwise from top:
The transparent glass walls of breakout and meeting areas reinforce a corporate culture based on principles of connection and communication. The reception area is just one of many double-height spaces designed to add airiness and expand sight lines. Quiet rooms offer spots for more focused work or confidential meetings. ➤

USER EXPERIENCE. LIFETIME VALUE. CONNECTED

0 20 40   80

1 LOUNGE AREA

2 MEETING ROOM

3 QUIET TIME ROOM

4 WORKSTATIONS

5 BREAKOUT HUB

6 DROP-IN/HOTELING

7 LOCKERS

PROJECT TEAM DUSHYANT JAIN, ADAM MUNDY,
LINDA ZEEMAN, SUPRATIM SENGUPTA, VICTOR WONG
PHOTOGRAPHY VITUS LAU/M MOSER

www.mmoser.com

Clockwise from opposite top: The "touchdown" area caters to mobile staffers, with "hot desk" hoteling stations. Café-style seating overlooks a lofty volume and the "boulevard" below. The lively eatery can accommodate 260 for sit-down meals or gatherings of up to 1,000. Vibrant colors and patterns keep the mood upbeat. Located at the base of the internal staircase, the boulevard doubles as a waiting area.

Dirk Denison Architects and Leslie Jones & Associates

CORPORATE OFFICE, CHICAGO

Clockwise from above: In the double-height reception, custom glass pendants illuminate a table of steel, stone, and glass. Frosted partitions screen administrative workstations from circulation routes. A hickory-clad volume houses support-staff facilities. ➤

A family-owned enterprise could suggest a certain casualness, but when this one approached Dirk Denison Architects and Leslie Jones & Associates to build its corporate headquarters, a degree of professional polish was required. The client also wanted a scheme that would create separation between each of three business divisions while allowing for shared meeting areas.

Rising 48 stories above Chicago's Loop, the office is a gemlike composition of hickory-clad and -trimmed facets that define conference rooms, executive offices, and administrative facilities for the senior staff. For the overall decor, millwork serves as a subtle leitmotif.

In addition to a dramatic staircase fashioned from stainless steel and glass, the light-filled reception is defined by hickory screens, one of which draws said light into the interior mezzanine. Upstairs, rich wood gives way to the dining room's hospitality-caliber finishes and furnishings (among the latter is a Henry Moore bronze, a highlight of a collection packed with masterworks). To accommodate these pieces—as well as others by Thomas Struth, Noriko Furunishi, Wolfgang Tilmans, Gilbert and George, and James Welling—generous circulation corridors provide intriguing sight lines and uninterrupted surfaces. A wise decision, since the client views its art holdings as part of the family.

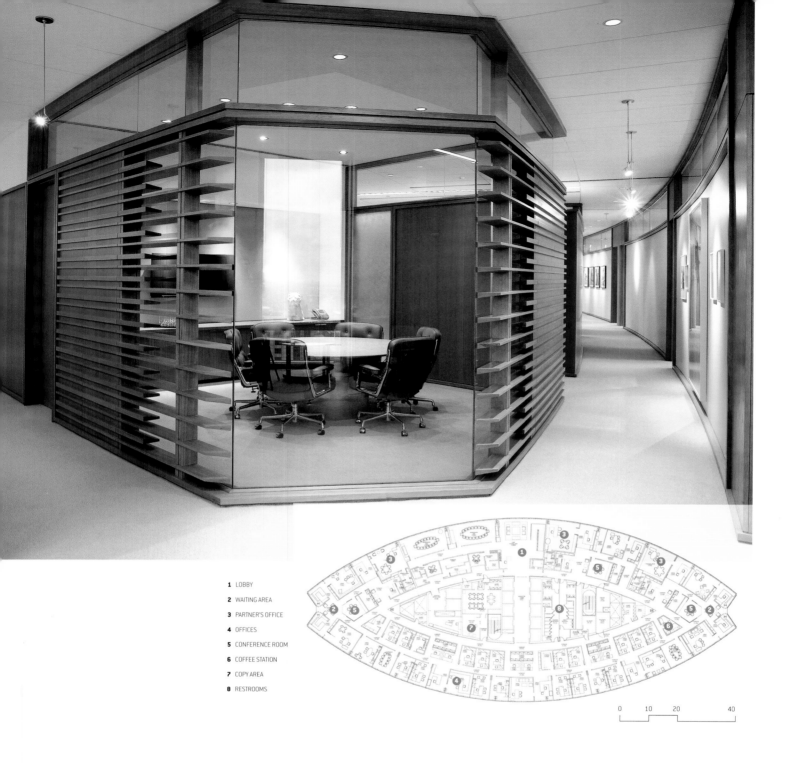

1 LOBBY

2 WAITING AREA

3 PARTNER'S OFFICE

4 OFFICES

5 CONFERENCE ROOM

6 COFFEE STATION

7 COPY AREA

8 RESTROOMS

0   10   20   40

PHOTOGRAPHY MICHELLE LITVIN (1, 2, 5, 6, 9, 11), SCOTT SHIGLEY (3, 4, 7, 8, 10)

www.dirkdenisonarchitects.com
www.ljai.com

33,000 sf
Floors 47 and 48

Clockwise from opposite top: Chairs by Charles and Ray Eames surround a conference room's limestone-top table. The dining area's George Nakashima walnut table, Henry Moore bronze, and Holly Hunt dining chairs. The screen motif extends to millwork detailing. A work by Wolfgang Tilmans anchors a hallway. A Thomas Struth photograph hangs next to reception's hickory staircase. Photographs by James Welling hang behind an Art Deco desk and Josef Hoffman guest chairs. Walter Knoll armchairs flank a piece by Gilbert and George. Museum-quality lighting shines on a series of James Welling photographs along a corridor.

Box Studios

SYBASE, AN SAP COMPANY
BROOMFIELD, COLORADO

If visitors entering Sybase's reception area—on the third floor of a LEED-Gold building—experience déja vu, there's good reason: That's precisely what Box Studios intended. The software company was accustomed to having its own building, and the architects wanted to create the illusion Sybase was still the sole tenant. How did the design team pull it off? By creating an entrance that subtly mimics the main lobby downstairs. The pale stone flooring is similar, as are the thin, linear light fixtures that march across the wood-clad ceiling. This approach reaped other benefits as well. "In Denver, a lot of lobbies are earthy and lodgelike," explains principal Lynn Coit, "but this one had a crisp, modern edge we wanted to bring into the space anyway."

Beyond the office's threshold, however, are plenty of truly singular design elements. The wood ceiling cuts a swath through the core and into the break room, where an intriguing mix of materials seeks to lure programmers from their computer screens. A backlit Interlam panel cascades down one wall, casting a soft glow on the dining surfaces below. Vertical-slit windows in the café walls let curious passersby peer inside without discomforting diners. Frosted window film applied to the center of the conference room's glass front similarly mitigates the fishbowl effect; in this case, visitors to reception are blocked from the distracting activities of ongoing meetings but treated to a grand view of the snowcapped mountain peaks beyond.

Clockwise from right: The reception area is wrapped in polished-limestone planks. A shimmery Interlam panel intersects the break room's woodlike ceiling (actually a faux bois Koroseal Arbor Series wall covering). The conference room and lobby are partially separated by a sculptural geometric wall, made with fin-and-strip millwork. The detail repeats on the break-room wall; bentwood LZF lamps pick up the motif overhead. Another view of the break room, with 9-inch-thick composite-slab tabletops.

PROJECT TEAM LYNN COIT, JIM GRACZYK, DANIELLE MEYER
PHOTOGRAPHY CHRIS ORWAT
www.bxstudios.com

28,014 sf

TOM ARBAN
www.tomarban.com

JOE C. AKER
www.akerimaging.com

CHRISTOPHER BARRETT
www.christopherbarrett.net

GABRIEL BENZUR
www.gbenzurphotography.com

MAGDA BIERNAT
www.magdabiernat.com

ROB BROWN
www.robbrownphoto.co.uk

DAVE BURK / HEDRICH BLESSING
www.hedrichblessing.com

BENNY CHAN / FOTOWORKS
www.fotoworks.cc

CHUCK CHOI
www.chuckchoi.com

CHRIS COOPER
www.chriscooperphotographer.com

DEBBIE FRANKE
debbie@debbiefranke.com

BRAD GILLETTE
www.bgillettephoto.com

HALKIN PHOTOGRAPHY
www.barryhalkin.com

STEVE HALL / HEDRICH BLESSING
www.hedrichblessing.com

GEORGE HEINRICH
www.heinrichphotography.com

RON JOHNSON
www.studio3301.com

JAIME JUSTINIANI
jaimejustiniani@gmail.com

NATHAN KIRKMAN
www.nathankirkman.com

ERIC LAIGNEL
www.ericlaignel.com

EDMON LEONG
www.edmonleong.com

MICHELLE LITVIN
www.michellelitvin.com

BJÖRG MAGNEA
www.bjorgmagnea.com

SCOTT McDONALD / HEDRICH BLESSING
www.hedrichblessing.com

NICK MERRICK / HEDRICH BLESSING
www.hedrichblessing.com

DAVID MOORE
www.moore-photo.com

CHRIS ORWAT
www.premiumdigitalsolutions.com

MICHAEL ROBINSON
www.mrobinsonphoto.com

JACK SHEA
www.sheastudio.com

SCOTT SHIGLEY
www.shigleyphoto.com

MELANIE SUGGS
706-264-7661

ANTHONY TAHLIER
www.anthonytahlier.com

PAUL WARCHOL
www.warcholphotography.com

DANA WHEELOCK
www.wheelockphotography.com

ADRIAN WILSON
www.interiorphotography.net

WILLIAM ZBAREN
www.zbaren.com

photographers index

INTERIOR DESIGN®

editor in chief Cindy Allen

EXECUTIVE EDITOR
Elena Kornbluth

DEPUTY EDITOR
Edie Cohen (West/Southwest)

ARTICLES EDITOR
Annie Block

SENIOR EDITORS
Mark McMenamin
Deborah Wilk

MANAGING EDITOR
Helene E. Oberman

EDITORIAL ASSISTANT
Matthew Powell

DESIGNERS
Zigeng Li
Karla Lima

ASSISTANT TO THE EDITOR IN CHIEF
Athena Waligore

BOOKS EDITOR
Stanley Abercrombie

EDITOR AT LARGE
Craig Kellogg

CONTRIBUTING EDITORS
Aric Chen
Cindy Coleman
Laura Fisher Kaiser
Raul Barreneche
Nicholas Tamarin

PRODUCTION MANAGER
Sarah Dentry / 646-805-0236 / sdentry@interiordesign.net

PREPRESS IMAGING SPECIALIST
Igor Tsiperson

RESEARCH DIRECTOR
Wing Leung / 646-805-0250

REPRINTS
Ness Feliciano / 708-660-8612 / fax 708-660-8613

INTERIORDESIGN.NET
ASSOCIATE WEB EDITOR
Meghan Edwards

ASSISTANT WEB EDITOR
Olivia Farquharson

CONTRIBUTING ONLINE EDITOR
Carlos Martinez-Jechevici

DESIGNWIRE DAILY CONTRIBUTORS
Arlene Hirst
Sara Pepitone
Andrew Stone
Ian Volner

SANDOW.
Brands Powered by Innovation™

chairman & ceo of sandow media Adam I. Sandow

CHIEF FINANCIAL OFFICER AND CHIEF OPERATING OFFICER
Chris Fabian

VICE PRESIDENT, CREATIVE AND EDITORIAL
Yolanda E. Yoh

VICE PRESIDENT, WEB TECHNOLOGY
Tom Cooper

VICE PRESIDENT, INFORMATION TECHNOLOGY
Jesus Sardinas

president Mark Strauss, hon. iida

ASSOCIATE PUBLISHER
Carol Cisco

DIGITAL MEDIA DIRECTOR
Pamela McNally

STRATEGIC AD DIRECTOR, NEW YORK
Gayle Shand

MARKETING DIRECTOR
Tina Brennan

EVENTS DIRECTOR
Rachel Long

ASSISTANT TO THE PRESIDENT
Kalyca Rei Murph

MARKETING
ART DIRECTOR
Denise Figueroa

SENIOR DESIGNERS
Selena Chen
Mihoko Miyata

SENIOR MANAGER
Yasmin Spiro

COORDINATOR
Andrea Rosen / 646-805-0277

INTERIORDESIGN.NET
DIGITAL MEDIA MANAGER
Ashley Walker

ASSISTANT WEB PRODUCER
Ashley Teater

SERVICES
HALL OF FAME DIRECTOR
Regina Freedman / 646-805-0270

CONTRACTS COORDINATOR
Sandy Campomanes / 646-805-0403

SPECIAL PROJECTS MANAGER
Kay Kojima / 646-805-0276

SALES
SALES REPRESENTATIVE
Kathy Harrigan / 646-805-0292

INTEGRATED MEDIA SALES
Karen Donaghy / 646-805-0291

INSIDE SALES DIRECTOR
Jonathan Kessler / 646-805-0279

SALES ASSOCIATE
Xiang Ping Zhu / 646-805-0269

SENIOR SALES COORDINATOR
Valentin Ortolaza / 646-805-0268

SALES ASSISTANT
Alana Taylor / 646-805-0271

PHILADELPHIA
Greg Kammerer / 610-738-7011 / fax 610-738-7195

ATLANTA, BUYERS GUIDE, E-SALES MANAGER
Craig Malcolm / 770-712-9245 / fax 770-234-5847

CHICAGO
Tim Kedzuch / 847-907-4050 / fax 847-556-6513
Julie McCarthy / 847-615-2077 / fax 847-713-4897

LOS ANGELES
Reed Fry / 949-223-1088 / fax 949-223-1089

FRANCE/GERMANY/POLAND
Mirek Kraczkowski / kraczko@aol.com / 48-22-401-7001 / fax 48-22-401-7016

ITALY
Riccardo Laureri / media@laureriassociates.it / 39-02-236-2500 / fax 39-02-236-4411

ASIA
Quentin Chan / quentinchan@leadingm.com / 852-2366-1106 / fax 852-2366-1107

AUDIENCE MARKETING SENIOR DIRECTOR
Katharine Tucker